Praise for *The Active Workday Advantage*

'Lizzie provides the inspiration and evidence-based tools you need to get moving and be your best, most productive self.'
Sophie Scott OAM, emotional wellbeing expert

'This book is not just a critique of the current system, but a practical guide to revolutionising our work lives. It's a must-read for anyone who believes in the possibility of a healthier, happier and more productive workplace.'
Chelsea Pottenger, founder and Director of EQ Minds

'In *The Active Workday Advantage*, Lizzie ignites the spirit of movement, infusing practical and enjoyable methods that invite everyone to participate. Her dynamism sparks immediate inspiration, reminding us that small changes can revolutionise our lives.'
Lynne Stockdale, Learning and Development Manager at Dexus

'With our people being our principal value creators, *The Active Workday Advantage* provides a blueprint for the future of work while illuminating the transformative power of an active workforce. This book brilliantly articulates how productivity, creativity and wellbeing intersect.'
Nathan Knight, Vice President and Managing Director of Hitachi Vantara Australia and New Zealand

'As someone who has suffered the consequences of bad posture and a decade of remote working, I only have one wish: that this book had come out twenty years ago. Read it. Practise it. Reinvent yourself.'
Phil Mershon, Director of Experience at Social Media Examiner and author of *Unforgettable*

'*The Active Workday Advantage* is the powerplay book in your back pocket every single day.'
Elka Whalan, dual Olympian, media presenter and founder of QueenHood

'Start with science, add enthusiasm, and you get Lizzie Williamson. Follow the guidance in this brilliant book and you'll banish sluggish from your vocab for good.'
Lucy Bloom, speaker, author and consultant

'I can see *The Active Workday Advantage* exceeding all expectations and changing lives and workplaces everywhere!'
Clare Stokes, Executive Assistant to the Supply Chain Officer at Super Retail Group

'This is a one-stop shop for shifting your mindset, dramatically improving your physical wellbeing and cutting out all the excuses for why you don't have time to take better care of yourself.'
Vashti Whitfield, resilience expert, filmmaker and author

'Want to work happier and live longer? *The Active Workday Advantage* is a superb collection of small acts that will transform how you work forever.'
Phil Hayes-St Clair, partnership expert, CEO and host of the *Partnership+ Podcast*

'This book is a breath of fresh air in the world of personal development. It's all the motivation you need to live your most effervescent and supercharged life!'
Lee Holmes, clinical nutritionist and author of ten books, including *Supercharged Food*

'*The Active Workday Advantage* is revolutionary in challenging sedentary habits. It's not just about work; it's about infusing life with vitality. Discovering strategies to incorporate movement seamlessly has revitalised my routine and reignited my motivation.'
Tracey Clark, Executive Assistant to the President at CHEP

'Lizzie's book is a constant reminder of the simple yet profound ways we can prioritise our mental health and wellbeing in the midst of our daily routines.'
Michelle Bowditch, CEO and founder of The Australian Assembly of Administrators and Door 20a

'I can confidently say that this book is a secret weapon for achieving a thriving career and a fulfilling life.'
Jessica Hickman, founder of Bullyology and author of *The Upstander Leader*

'*The Active Workday Advantage* is not another generic guide to living a healthier life; it's a treasure trove of innovative ideas and practical advice that can truly transform your relationship with the sedentary nature of work and life.'
Yasmin London, Director of Digital Resilience, APAC, at Linewize ANZ

'*The Active Workday Advantage* is not only a great and timely idea, it's just what the doctor ordered!'
Matthew Johnstone, Director of Drawn from Experience

'Lizzie creates fun, loving movement in a busy work or desk day to help our overall wellbeing – mentally and physically.'
Michele Chevalley Hedge, wellbeing author and presenter on positive psychology and nutritional medicine

‘As a self-confessed lazy desk lump, I love these straightforward, doable ideas on how to create more movement in my everyday. Now, where did I put my leg warmers?’

Kate Toon, entrepreneur and author of *Six Figures in School Hours*

‘*The Active Workday Advantage* is a compilation of achievable and practical micro-habits that you can implement to power up your performance in the digital, sedentary world we now live and work in.’

Dr Kristy Goodwin, author of *Dear Digital, We need to talk*

‘With simple, quick and easy ways to get moving in our day, Lizzie’s book is an absolute game-changer for life and work.’

Libby Allaway, corporate stylist, author, speaker and client experience creator

‘Lizzie’s infectious energy, brilliant writing and insanely doable hacks is a winning formula.’

Amelia Phillips, nutritionist and exercise scientist

‘Lizzie transformed how I blend my workouts and workday, bought joy back into my fitness breaks and helped me to come home to my body.’

Amy Molloy, editor and author of *The World is a Nice Place*

‘Lizzie brings her trademark energy and insight into something that will absolutely improve your physical and mental health.’

Jason Thompson, content coach, keynote speaker and founder of SpeakUp Get Results

‘This book brought me so many new ideas, but also helped me understand why I was feeling the way I was. I highly recommend it to everyone.’

Amy Taylor-Kabbaz, host of the *Happy Mama Movement Podcast* and author of *Mama Rising*

‘Lizzie’s easy-to-implement frameworks will take you from exhausted to energised – elevating your wellbeing and improving your overall productivity.’

Michelle Broadbent, business strategist and host of the *Your Business Boost* podcast

‘Packed full of practical advice and the usual Lizzie fun, this is a must read for anyone looking to improve their energy, productivity and experience of work.’

Matt Cowdroy, CEO and productivity ninja at Think Productive Australia/NZ

THE ACTIVE WORKDAY ADVANTAGE

The Active Workday Advantage

Unlock your most energised, engaged and happy self at work

Lizzie Williamson

MACMILLAN

To Stella and Ruby.
Dream big.
Start small.

First published in 2024 by Major Street Publishing Pty Ltd

First published in India 2024 by Macmillan
an imprint of Pan Macmillan Publishing India Private Limited
707 Kailash Building
26 K. G. Marg, New Delhi 110001
www.panmacmillan.co.in

Pan Macmillan, The Smithson, 6 Briset Street, Farringdon, London EC1M 5NR
Associated companies throughout the world
www.panmacmillan.com

ISBN 978-93-6113-288-9

1 3 5 7 9 8 6 4 2

Internal design by Production Works
Printed and bound by Gopsons Papers Pvt. Ltd., Noida

Contents

Preface

One day, when my daughter Ruby was 15 years old, she came home from school in a terrible mood. Thumping her heavy schoolbag on the table, she said to me, 'I don't understand why we have to sit for six hours straight listening to teacher after teacher, class after class. We're all falling asleep. We can't concentrate. My back is so sore. Why do we have to sit so much? Why is school designed this way?'

'I have no idea!' I said to her. 'But I'm writing a book about the same thing, except in the workplace, hoping that more people will start to ask these questions too. When you enter the workforce, Ruby, I want things to be different.'

Have you ever stopped and thought: *Why are we working and learning for hours in a sedentary way when we know it's not good for us, both physically and mentally? Why has it become the norm in our workdays to sit and sit and sit?*

We're designed to move and be active, yet we confine ourselves to chairs and desks for hours on end. Our bodies and minds suffer the consequences of this prolonged inactivity and we experience aches and pains, decreased focus and diminished productivity.

The current norm of sitting for long hours, immobile and disconnected from our bodies, is deeply ingrained in our work culture, but it's time to challenge the status quo and ask ourselves why we accept it. Why do we spend our days confined to chairs, neglecting our physical and mental wellbeing?

It's partly because spending hours working statically aligns with our idea of success, which is to be productive, get results and achieve the accolades that come with the grind we've glorified. The harder we work, the more hours we put in, the fewer breaks we take and the more we produce, achieve and deliver. But you only have to look at the rate of burnout, the rise of physical and mental health issues and other concerning trends to wonder: *Is this really working? Is there a better way?*

I want my daughters' workdays to look vastly different when they grow up. I envision a future in which they don't have to battle the negative effects of sedentary behaviour or suffer from the physical and mental strains of prolonged sitting. Instead, I want them to work in an active way that brings them energy, engagement and joy.

And I want this for you too.

I know it's possible because I've seen it firsthand. I've seen what happens when individuals break up long hours of sitting by embracing movement and wellbeing in the workplace. I've seen movement incorporated seamlessly into the fabric of the workday and I've seen the transformative results that follow.

Whether you're reading this book because you're an employee who feels constantly exhausted, you're a working parent who feels overwhelmed, you're a manager who wants to raise morale or you work in human resources and you want to be a role model for change, I applaud you. You're here because, like me, you can see the faults of the system – the unsustainability of expecting people to perform without nurturing their physical and mental wellbeing – and you want to fix them.

This book is a call to action to shift our perspective and prioritise our health and vitality in the workplace. It's a plea to employers, employees and sole traders alike to recognise the immense value of incorporating movement into our workdays.

Are you ready to challenge the norms, rewrite the rules and create a new narrative for our working lives? Let's reimagine, redesign and revolutionise how we work, one small step at a time. Let's go!

Lizzie

The warm-up

Imagine a workday with access to a pharmacy filled with all the pills and potions you need to feel energised, focused and fulfilled. Picture yourself strolling through the aisles, selecting elixirs that enhance your brainpower, boost your memory and ignite your creativity. Better still, it's all free! You'd be there without hesitation, right?

Guess what? You don't need a magical pharmacy to access these transformative benefits. Nope, you already possess an incredible power within you. Think of it as your very own wellbeing laboratory, just waiting to be tapped into.

The secret to unlocking this new level of productivity, focus and fulfilment? Embracing something simple, yet incredibly powerful: an active workday. By integrating more movement into your work routine, you have the power to elevate your wellbeing, increase your cognitive abilities and cause a profound shift in how you approach and engage with your work.

Now, before you dismiss this idea with an excuse – perhaps, 'There is no way I have the time to exercise during my workday. Have you seen my inbox?!' – let me assure you that you won't find in these pages any suggestions to overhaul your entire routine or sacrifice precious work hours. You might even say, 'I already exercise outside of work'. That's fantastic! However, research shows that even if you hit the gym before work or exercise after hours, it's not enough to counteract the adverse effects of prolonged sitting if you spend the rest of your day sedentary. That's why incorporating physical activity into your workday is crucial for your overall wellbeing. And the rest of your excuses? Get ready to have them busted in the following chapters – there's a reason I've been dubbed 'the excuse-buster from Down Under'!

As you journey through this book, you'll realise that an active workday isn't a temporary fix or passing trend. It's sustainable and transformative – and it has the capacity to revolutionise your work life. Whether you're an executive seeking to optimise your team's performance, a manager striving to foster a culture of wellbeing or an employee yearning for a more energised and fulfilling workday, *The Active Workday Advantage* will give you the practical steps and strategies to reimagine, redesign and revolutionise your professional life.

From reimagining to a revolution

In the first part of *The Active Workday Advantage* we're challenging the status quo. I'm going to help you shift your mindset, break free from restrictive rules and reimagine both exercise and your workday. By daring to think differently, you'll unlock the true potential of exercise and discover how it can enhance your productivity and wellbeing. It's time to rewrite the rules, remove common roadblocks and redefine what exercise means to you.

We'll also tackle something you might already be feeling: resistance. Don't worry – it's a natural response when we introduce change and interrupt old habits and routines. But here's the exciting part: change doesn't have to mean a complete overhaul. We'll explore how small, manageable adjustments can be effective, making it easy for you to embrace this transformation without feeling overwhelmed.

Adopting a new approach is one thing, but making it a lasting part of our lives is another. We'll explore practical strategies that are both simple and effective to solidify your new routines. I'll show you how to harness the power of accountability and create an environment to champion your wellbeing. You'll also learn clever techniques to make your active habits stick.

With a shift in mindset and a taste of what's possible, we'll then dive into redesigning our workday from sedentary to active.

The science-backed moments of movement and rejuvenation you'll discover in the second part of this book will change how you feel and perform throughout the day for the better. From brief stretches to mindful breathing exercises and energising activities, these micro moves will refresh and revitalise your work routine. As your workday transforms before your eyes, you'll wonder why you didn't question your sedentary habits before.

As we step into part III, we'll delve into the heart of the active workday revolution. This revolution centres on transforming the workplace into a cornerstone for healthier habits, fostering increased engagement and enhancing the workday experience. By harnessing the power of movement and uniting our teams, we'll set a clear vision and work towards tangible milestones. The roadmap serves as our guiding blueprint, turning the active workplace revolution into a reality. By the end of this journey, you'll emerge as a pivotal force in this revolution, elevating both productivity and wellbeing in your workplace.

Together, we'll make the active workday a natural and integral part of working life. Get ready to experience the active workday advantage!

Part I
Reimagine
The active workday idea

The active workday idea invites you to reimagine how you approach your workday. In a world where sedentary lifestyles have become the norm, the active workday sets out to challenge this status quo by breaking up long periods of sitting with purposeful and strategic moments of movement.

In the pages that follow, you'll discover precisely why guidelines for physical activity and sedentary behaviour recommend that you minimise prolonged, inactive sitting and break up these lengthy sitting sessions as often as you can. You'll have your eyes opened to the multitude of advantages this provides, in both the long term and the short term. Change isn't always easy, though. Roadblocks and resistance often impede progress. Your journey will involve navigating these challenges, fostering new mindsets and uncovering the strategies that will make an active workday your reality.

Work and wellbeing don't have to be mutually exclusive. In the second part of this book – 'Redesign: The active workday toolkit' – you'll find a selection of 'micro moves' to choose from to create your own active workday. These moves, which can take as little as a few seconds or minutes to execute, are powerful catalysts. They invigorate not only the body but also the mind, putting you at an advantage. The ideas you'll encounter here in 'Reimagine: The active workday idea' will pave the way for you to fully embrace the toolkit, making it easy and enjoyable to seamlessly integrate movement into your daily routine.

If you've ever wanted to breathe fresh life into your workday, reshape your relationship with physical activity or reignite your motivation, these next five chapters will set you up to do just that. Together we'll uncover practical strategies to make positive changes that will infuse more vitality into your workday and your life as a whole.

1 The reasons

Why the way we work needs to change

Change the changeable, accept the unchangeable, and remove yourself from the unacceptable

Denis Waitley

As I step up to the mic, I can't help but hear a few groans escape from the audience. It's a sound I've become all too familiar with when I take the stage at workplaces and conferences.

Why do the groans happen? It's because people know I'm about to ask them to do something they don't want to do. And I get it. It's natural to feel resistance to getting off our chairs and moving our bodies – especially when we're asked to do it in a room full of our co-workers.

For over a decade, I've worked with organisations around the world to help their employees re-energise their bodies and revitalise their minds. Whenever I do a talk or workshop, I always lead my audience in a series of 'micro moves' – a kind of mini exercise break where I get people up on their feet and encourage them to stretch, move, dance and get their blood flowing.

The feedback is always amazing, but I won't lie: the initial reactions aren't always enthusiastic. The groans I hear reflect the resistance we naturally feel when confronted with the idea of breaking free from our comfortable seats. When I look out at the audience, I see it in their faces – the hesitation and reluctance to disrupt long hours of sitting, even though they know they should.

Paying the price: the cost of inactivity

We've heard it from doctors, governments and countless health organisations. The evidence is clear: sitting less and moving more is essential for our overall wellbeing. Yet, despite this knowledge, many of us still find ourselves trapped in chair-bound workdays and pay the price for our inactivity.

When we spend hours glued to our chairs, barely moving a muscle, our bodies rebel with aches, pains and stiffness. We feel the consequences emotionally, too, and our performance suffers. Our creativity dwindles, our focus wanes and that feeling of being physically in the room but mentally disengaged – a state aptly dubbed 'languishing' by organisational psychologist Adam Grant – sets in. Stress levels rise, cortisol wreaks havoc on our health and burnout becomes an all-too-real threat.

Behind a seemingly harmless desk-bound routine lies an array of health risks that build silently with each passing sedentary day. Studies have consistently linked prolonged sitting to an increased risk of obesity, heart disease, diabetes and even certain types of cancer. The body, designed for movement and activity, rebels when forced into a sedentary state. The metabolism slows down, muscles weaken and circulation becomes compromised, setting the stage for a cascade of health challenges. As Dr James A Levine writes, 'Sitting is more dangerous than smoking ... We are sitting ourselves to death.'

Perhaps one of the most compelling revelations of current research is the link between a sedentary lifestyle and a shortened lifespan. The evidence is sobering. Studies have shown that each hour spent sitting, particularly while engaging in screen-based activities, can eat away at our physical health and accumulate to take years off our lives.

You might think that hitting the gym before or after work offers a protective shield against the harmful effects of prolonged sitting. However, research reveals that this assumption is far from accurate. While regular exercise undoubtedly yields numerous health benefits, it doesn't negate the effects of prolonged sitting. The health risks associated with hours spent at a desk still accumulate, regardless of our commitment to fitness outside of work.

The impact extends beyond the individual, too. It ripples through society, affecting the economy, our relationships and our overall quality of life. Worse still, we fall under the collective delusion that this is the only way that work – and life – can feel. *This is just what 'adulting' feels like*, we tell ourselves. But does it have to be that way? (Spoiler alert: the answer is no!)

Let me be the person to give you permission to want more, the person who says you don't have to feel terrible just because you're an adult! You can have a full-time job and achieve your dreams *without* sacrificing your physical and mental health. Of course, we all face health challenges during our lives, but these are different to the aches, pains and ailments caused by our lifestyles and our socially ingrained way of working. What if I told you that vitality is a human right – and you can access it?

The knowing–doing gap

Every one of the thousands of employees, managers, leaders and business owners I speak to each year is aware of at least some of the costs of a sedentary work life. They know that humans need to be physically active; they know that lack of physical activity negatively affects their physical and mental health. The reality, however, is that we can know all these things and not do anything about them. Why is that?

In our daily lives, so many things get in our way. We tell ourselves that we don't have the time. There are always deadlines to meet, never-ending emails to reply to and back-to-back meetings that go on for too long. No wonder physical activity often goes to the bottom of an already oversized to-do list. We can't find the motivation or energy, so we say we'll do it tomorrow, next week, next month. We hate the thought of exercise – it's too uncomfortable or embarrassing – so we find any excuse not to do it.

Igniting the spark

The resistance I witness when I stand on stage and gaze out at a sea of faces is extremely common – and perfectly natural. But every time I get people on their feet and moving, a remarkable transformation occurs. The same individuals who were initially hesitant – even those who groaned! – begin to change.

Admittedly, people may feel a touch of self-consciousness during this temporary departure from their comfort zone, but this feeling quickly gives way as the power of movement takes hold. Uncertain smiles become confident and contagious, and the room fills with energy. What I hear most often from people afterwards is a heartfelt, 'Thank you, I feel so much better', and often, 'I feel like a new person! I needed that'.

The truth is, amid the pressures of our workdays, we all need those precious moments of joy, vitality and centredness. Think about it: how often do you feel stuck, mentally exhausted or lacking in inspiration? How often have you wished for a boost of energy, a surge of creativity or a clearer mind to tackle your tasks and challenges? How often do you wish your body felt less tight and achy? These are the moments when an active workday could become your greatest ally.

Picture a workday in which you feel not just awake but genuinely refreshed and inspired. Your body feels open, strong and comfortable. Your brain is firing on all cylinders, ideas flowing like a river. You navigate through your tasks with ease, handling annoying colleagues and negative emotions with a calm demeanour. Stress and anxiety are present, but they're no longer drowning you – they're manageable. Imagine yourself at your desk, a genuine smile on your face, radiating a contagious positive mindset.

Why are you so happy? Why are you so engaged in what you're doing? It's as if you've discovered the secret to a perfect workday. You feel connected to those around you, whether in the room or online. You're not just getting through your tasks – you're truly living in each moment. And here's the best part: you can see the ripple effect of your vitality. Your health, happiness and energy are not contained within the office walls; they spill over into your life outside of work, positively affecting those you care about.

Now, let's introduce the vehicle of this transformation: breaking up prolonged sitting with physical activity. Yes, you read that right. The simple act of moving your body has the power to turn this dream into reality. It's not just wishful thinking; it's backed by science. The profound impact of physical activity on mood, physical health and mental wellbeing is no longer a secret – it's within your grasp.

An active workday can transform your life

So, what exactly happens inside us when we move? An ever-growing body of research is uncovering the profound effects of physical activity on our bodies, brains and mental health. Renowned experts such as New York University neuroscientist Wendy Suzuki emphasise that exercise is 'the most transformative thing that you can do for your brain today'.

Our ancestors engaged in physical activities essential for survival in the vast landscapes they roamed, thriving on the profound bond between their bodies and minds. Our brains evolved and developed to their full potential through movement. This deep-rooted connection between movement and optimal brain function is ingrained in our DNA, shaping who we are today.

As we get moving, our bodies awaken ancient magic within us. It's as if our ancestors left us a secret recipe for wellbeing – and all we have to do is combine the ingredients. With each step we take and each move we make, our bodies respond in the most remarkable ways. A symphony of chemicals and hormones is performed inside us.

From resistance to rewards: accessing your inner pharmacy

Welcome to the Active Workday Pharmacy, where you optimise your experience at work by harnessing the power of movement. As you engage in physical activity, you gain access to its aisles of magical ingredients that can transform your workday.

Aisle 1: brain power boosters – elevate your cognitive performance

In aisle 1, brain power boosters await to nourish your mind and elevate your cognitive abilities. One key ingredient, brain-derived neurotrophic factor (BDNF), plays a crucial role. This protein enhances communication between brain cells and even helps to make new brain cells. Decreased levels of BDNF are associated with Parkinson's disease and Alzheimer's disease. As you move, your BDNF levels increase, leading to improved problem-solving skills, heightened creativity and enhanced adaptability. By optimising your brain's functioning, you unlock greater productivity and innovation in your work.

Aisle 2: serotonin shields – fortify yourself against stress

Aisle 2 is home to serotonin shields that help to fortify you against stress. Serotonin, a neurotransmitter, plays a significant role in regulating mood and emotional wellbeing. Physical activity triggers the release of serotonin, which fosters emotional resilience, decreases anxiety and enhances your ability to cope with stress by providing a shield against the negative effects of cortisol, the stress hormone. This natural biochemical balance helps you navigate challenges with composure and maintain a positive outlook on your work.

Aisle 3: relaxation remedies – discover calm amid the chaos

When work becomes overwhelming, head to aisle 3, where relaxation remedies await. One notable remedy is the chill pill, otherwise known as endocannabinoids, which interacts with receptors in your brain, promoting feelings of tranquillity and wellbeing. Physical activity stimulates the production and release of endocannabinoids, allowing you to find moments of calm amid the chaos of your workday. By embracing movement and partaking in these remedies, you attain a clear and relaxed mind, enabling you to approach your tasks with renewed focus and productivity.

Aisle 4: motivation elixirs – ignite your inner drive

In aisle 4, motivation elixirs await. Dopamine, a neurotransmitter associated with reward and pleasure, is the key ingredient in these elixirs. As you engage in physical activity, your dopamine levels rise, activating your brain's reward pathways. This surge of satisfaction and joy fuels your motivation and passion for work. Tasks feel more enjoyable and fulfilling, driving you to pursue your professional goals with enthusiasm and determination.

Aisle 5: energy tonics – sustain your vitality throughout the day

Aisle 5 is where energy tonics await to revitalise your energy levels. Physical activity triggers the release of endorphins, neurotransmitters known for their euphoric effects and pain-reducing properties. These endorphin-infused tonics combat fatigue and replenish your natural vigour. By sipping on these tonics, you restore and sustain your energy levels, allowing you to stay focused, engaged and productive throughout the day.

Aisle 6: connection potions – foster collaboration and team spirit

Connection potions are stored in aisle 6. These potions combine oxytocin, the social bonding hormone, with myokines. Nicknamed 'hope molecules' by scientists, myokines are released during muscle contractions and promote unity and cooperation. Physical activity triggers the release of oxytocin and myokines, enhancing social connections and fostering a sense of trust and camaraderie. By partaking in these potions, you experience increased cooperation and collaboration, and a more positive work culture.

Action time! Activate your aspirations

Take a moment to reflect on what you could gain from the Active Workday Pharmacy. In this book, we'll delve into the specifics of the movements, mindsets and moments that can enhance our workdays.

Consider the areas of your life that could benefit the most if you access the pharmacy within you. Are you seeking increased focus and cognitive performance? Do you long for stress resilience and emotional balance? Perhaps you crave sustained energy and vitality or deeper connection and collaboration with your colleagues. Take note of your aspirations, and in the following chapters we'll uncover the strategies and practices that will empower you to achieve your goals.

Let's get physical: the physiological wonders that await

For an extra boost of motivation, it's worth taking a moment to remember that physical activity offers more than immediate benefits – it's critical to unlocking your long-term physical potential. Let's dive into the physiological wonders that await us when we move our bodies.

Pump up your heart: cardiovascular marvels

Engaging in physical activity turns our hearts into rock stars thanks to a process called 'cardiovascular adaptation'. Our hearts work harder when we exercise, pumping fresh blood with newfound vigour. Over time, the muscles of our hearts grow more robust. This increased strength ensures the efficient circulation of oxygen and vital nutrients throughout our bodies, benefiting every organ and tissue. Not only does this boost our endurance and athletic performance, but it also keeps our arteries clear and free from fatty build-up, reducing the risk of heart disease and other cardiovascular conditions.

Burn, baby, burn: metabolism on fire

When we get moving, our bodies transform into calorie-burning machines. Physical activity activates our metabolism, the complex chemical process that converts food into energy. Aerobic exercises in particular enhance the efficiency of our metabolic system, increasing the rate at which we burn calories, even at rest. This heightened metabolic state helps us manage our weight and body composition, as excess calories are used rather than stored as fat. Regular physical activity not only helps us achieve and maintain a healthy weight but also contributes to improved overall metabolic health, reducing the risk of metabolic disorders such as type 2 diabetes and obesity.

Unleashing your inner strength: muscle power

Physical activity sets in motion a remarkable process known as 'muscle adaptation'. When we challenge our muscles through resistance training, they undergo microscopic tears. Our bodies are incredible machines that respond to these challenges by repairing and rebuilding the muscle fibres, making them stronger and more resilient. This process, which is called 'muscle hypertrophy', increases the size and number of muscle cells. The result is improved muscular strength, power and endurance. Regular exercise helps us perform daily tasks more easily and contributes to increased athletic performance, reduced risk of injuries and enhanced overall functional capacity.

Building strong foundations: bone health basics

Let's not forget about our bones. Physical activity is essential for building and maintaining optimal bone health. Weight-bearing exercises, such as walking and weightlifting, subject our bones to mechanical stress. In response, our bodies initiate a process called 'bone remodelling'. During this process, bone tissue is broken down and rebuilt, resulting in stronger and denser bones, which reduces the risk of osteoporosis and fractures. By strengthening our skeletal system, we enhance our mobility, maintain posture and improve our overall quality of life as we age.

Aging with grace: defying stiffness and embracing vitality

Speaking of aging, here's a secret to aging gracefully: regular physical activity. As we age, our bodies naturally experience a decline in flexibility, joint mobility and overall range of motion. An active lifestyle, however, can help defy stiffness and maintain vitality. Regular stretching exercises, movement and activities promoting mobility can preserve our joint health, flexibility and overall physical function.

You've probably seen those amazing elderly influencers on social media who are busting out dance moves in their 80s, running marathons in their 90s and generally living the 'third acts' of their lives to the fullest. Well, they don't have to be a minority. I believe, and science agrees, that we can all access more energy and vitality than we do in the average day, and this can energise not only our workdays but also our entire lives.

Core points

- Sitting is the new smoking. Your chair may be costing you more than you think, from health issues to creativity slumps.
- The gym alone won't save you. Sweating it out at the gym is great, but it won't erase the risk of extended hours glued to your desk.
- Resistance to movement is natural. People often resist physical activity, especially in a workplace setting.
- There is another way: choose an active workday! Embrace movement as your secret weapon, enhancing energy, creativity and fulfillment at work.
- Your inner pharmacy awaits. Movement ignites the magical ingredients to transform your workday – and your life.

2

The roadblocks

Obstacles as opportunities

When obstacles arise, you change your direction to reach your goal; you do not change your decision to get there.
Zig Ziglar

When I was growing up, every morning before school you'd find me in my family's garage doing my pliés (knee bends in ballet) at my little barre. I could easily dance and move for hours. That feeling of joy and energy from being active led me to become a professional dancer, dancing around the world, doing the cancan at casinos and performing in chorus lines on cruise ships.

Life took an unexpected turn in 2008. Despite my love for movement, I found myself unable to engage in the very activity that had always brought me happiness. I had a beautiful baby and a delightful toddler, but I had become trapped in a state of despair, consumed by guilt and shame. My mind was haunted by dark and truly terrifying thoughts that only added to the weight I carried. The positive, action-oriented person I once knew had been lost.

I knew deep down that I should prioritise exercise and physical activity, but my exhaustion and demanding schedule were barriers that seemed insurmountable. The motivation I once possessed dwindled to an all-time low. Everything, especially exercise, felt way too hard.

I found myself waiting – waiting for a solution that would magically fix everything. Of course, that didn't arrive. As my emotions spiralled and I hurtled towards rock bottom, I finally sought help from my doctor. She diagnosed me with postnatal depression, presented me with treatment options and, as I was about to leave her office, said one last thing: 'When you get on a plane, they tell you that in an emergency you have to put on your oxygen mask before assisting others. That's what you have to do.'

With her words echoing in my mind, I went home thinking about how this oxygen mask thing could possibly work for me. I didn't have the time. I felt too tired. It all felt hopeless and impossible. However, sometimes you arrive at a point in life when you must drill down to find a source of energy to help you overcome your challenges. You must dig deeper than you thought possible and summon the grit and courage you forgot you had. This was that moment for me.

The next day I went to my kitchen bench and put my hands on it like it was my barre. Even though it felt so, *so* hard, I did a plié. And then I did another. And another. Plié after plié.

All I could get myself to do on that first day was a couple of minutes, and my mind told me that that was a pointless amount of time. However, my heart told me differently. I felt two things I hadn't felt for months – a tiny flicker of hope and a small sense of achievement. Here was something that none of my excuses or obstacles could get in the way of me doing. And that was enough to bring me back the next day, and the next day. I committed to doing two minutes of movement every day. Those two precious minutes of exercise became my lifeline. I'm not exaggerating when I tell you that that habit and the ripple effect it created – seeking more professional help, reaching out to friends, making both my physical and mental fitness a priority – saved my life.

Be your own excuse buster

As I slowly started to recover, one small step at a time, I began to realise that certain mindsets I had towards exercise had been getting in my way of using it as the powerful tool it is. Over the next decade, I went on to build a global movement – Two Minute Moves – to help others change their perspective on exercise and make it possible when it *feels* impossible. As I discovered, it was much needed. It proved life-changing for many of the people I shared my message with.

However, adoption wasn't always seamless. Time and time again I spoke to people facing roadblocks to being active, especially at work. Many of these people knew it was one of the best things they could be doing, but they were finding it way too hard to start. Life is full of roadblocks, detours and unexpected turns. As we navigate our complex modern lives, these obstacles can hinder – or even completely derail – our pursuit of an active workday. It's easy to get trapped in a cycle of excuses and limitations that holds us back from embracing movement as an integral part of our daily routine.

What I learned from my own journey, as well as from years of research and insightful conversations with experts and individuals in the workplace, is that at every roadblock there is an opportunity for a mindset makeover. The perception of having no time, lacking motivation or being too tired to be active can all be reframed as calls for creative solutions. Just as a detour redirects your journey, these challenges can redirect your approach to movement.

As we dive into this world of roadblocks and excuses, we must first acknowledge that not everyone can engage in all types of movement. You may have ailments, injuries, disabilities or chronic pain, for example. Perhaps you're experiencing the weight of depression and high levels of stress or anxiety, making it challenging to take action. You are not alone. You don't have to suffer in silence. Seek professional help. By no means do the suggestions in this book supersede the advice or support of medical professionals.

You may not be as fit, strong, able-bodied, flexible or supple as you used to be, but you know what? That's perfectly okay. Honour your body and state of mind, and do what you can. Progress comes in all shapes and sizes, and every effort counts. What I want to focus on is what you *can* do and help you overcome the roadblocks you might face in accessing moments of movement and their benefits. We can all come up with a million reasons why we're the one person who can't make a change. It is, however, possible to override that voice in your head saying you're too busy, too tired, too stressed out or too unfit. You'll probably surprise yourself!

Picture yourself as a superhero with the word 'excuse' emblazoned across your chest. You've earned the title 'The Excuse Buster'. (This is a moniker that was bestowed upon me by the US media, and I'll pass it to you now.) Whenever you feel the inclination to make excuses for yourself, don your Excuse Buster outfit (just like Clark Kent transforming into Superman in a phone booth) and unleash the superhero that your body, brain and spirit yearn for. Watch out for the 'TRY THIS' sections to put the principles and ideas covered in this book into action.

Excuse buster 1: break the exercise rules

The first roadblock I'd like to address concerns a common mindset that goes like this: I'm not going to be able to find an hour to exercise today. I've got way too much work to do to make it to the gym or attend my Pilates class and I can't get out for a walk today. I'll just have to wait until tomorrow, the next day or the one after that.

This is what is known as the 'all-or-nothing' mindset. It's the belief that if exercise doesn't align with our preconceived notions of what it should look like – be that in tems of time, specific location, intensity, equipment or results – then it's not worth doing. Then, when we can't meet those rigid expectations of what exercise *should* look like, what do we end up doing? Nothing at all.

But how did we first arrive at this specific concept of exercise?

A (very) short history of exercise

If we look back, physical activity used to be an integral part of our daily tasks and routines. We engaged in activities such as hunting and gathering, tending to livestock, chopping firewood and washing our clothes by hand. These activities provided us with the necessary movement and energy expenditure to maintain good health. No one ever exercised just for their health.

However, as our lives became more comfortable and sedentary, often with the help of technology, the need to offset this shift became apparent. As office jobs became the norm, our awareness of health benefits associated with regular physical activity grew and exercise became essential. Enter the era of special equipment, fancy activewear and the latest must-do fitness classes, all of which have contributed to the rise of the US$96 billion global fitness industry.

Here's the truth: your body and brain don't care about the rules that you (or the fitness industry) set about what exercise should look like. They don't care if you're in fancy workout attire or have expensive equipment. There is no Exercise Police telling you what counts as exercise. Your body and brain simply want you to move in any way possible, because that's how they thrive and function at their best. They just want you to sit a bit less and move a bit more.

From all-or-nothing to all-or-something

Next time you tell yourself you can't get active because it doesn't match what you think exercise has to look like, turn that all-or-nothing mindset into an all-or-*something* mindset. Something is much better than nothing.

As you'll discover in the second part of this book, physical activity doesn't have to be confined to specific times or places, such as dedicated gym sessions or structured workout routines. Rather, movement can be woven seamlessly into the very fabric of your workday. Whether it's quick stretching exercises at your desk or taking little breaks for movement (or 'micro moves' – more on these soon) between tasks, the possibilities are endless. By flipping the all-or-nothing mindset to an all-or-*something* mindset, exercise can become a natural and effortless component of your day, allowing you to reap the benefits without disrupting your workflow or making you feel overwhelmed.

It also helps to be aware that when we're under stress or feeling anxious we tend to fall into black-and-white thinking: this is right, this is wrong, this is good, this is bad. An all-or-something mindset, in contrast, celebrates the whole spectrum of activities and emotions we can do and feel in life. I find that it's also helpful to look at the bigger picture over the longer term. If you don't do any exercise over the next three months, it will add up to nada. However, if you do just two minutes of exercise a day, it will add up to almost 200 minutes – and that's not nothing!

Excuse buster 2: change your relationship with exercise

For many of us, the word 'exercise' holds negative connotations. We associate exercise with feeling unfit and sweaty and, quite frankly, it's something we hate. For some it brings back unhappy memories of school sports or uncomfortable experiences of feeling out of place at the gym.

Unfortunately, I've had my own experience of an unhappy relationship with exercise. When I worked on a cruise ship as a dancer I was told that I needed to lose weight. From that horrible moment, exercise became something I used to punish and 'fix' my body. It took over ten years to change this perspective and use exercise to help the way I felt rather than looked.

In *Exercised: The science of physical activity, rest and health*, Daniel Lieberman writes, 'While the word has long been used to denote practising or training to improve skills or health, to be "exercised" also means to be harassed, vexed or worried about something'. During my 15 years as a personal trainer I heard my fair share of horror stories from clients about their past experiences with exercise.

Change the word, change your world

If the word 'exercise' is holding you back, let's change it. Picture swapping out two letters in the word 'exercise' so it becomes 'energise'. Compare 'I need to *exercise* today' to 'I need to *energise* today' and 'How do I *exercise* at work?' to 'How do I *energise* at work?' Feel different?

Think of your heart as a diligent worker, tirelessly pumping blood and oxygen to fuel your body's every move. Now, imagine it becoming a superhero with regular physical activity. As you get active, your heart gets a workout of its own. It strengthens and becomes a more efficient blood-pumping machine. Think of it as a muscle gaining strength. This enhanced cardiovascular health comes with a remarkable perk: it saves you energy.

When your heart is in tip-top shape, it doesn't have to labour as hard to deliver the oxygen and nutrients your body craves. It's like having a high-performance sports car instead of an old clunker. With this newfound efficiency, your daily activities become easier, and you have more energy left in your tank for your work and the things you love.

That's not all. When you get active, your lungs join the party. They kick into high gear, taking in more oxygen with every breath. This oxygen is the lifeblood of your muscles, fuelling them to work their magic and create energy through a process called 'aerobic metabolism'. It's like giving your muscles a turbo boost.

What's the outcome of better oxygen delivery creating happier muscles that are ready to work better and for longer? You feel more energetic and alive, all thanks to your heart and lungs teaming up to power your workday. Don't let a negative association with a word get in your way of all these incredible benefits in your workday and beyond.

In chapter 10, which focuses on vitalising your energy, you'll find lots of micro moves you can use to put this idea into practice.

Excuse buster 3: rethink time

The World Health Organization recommends that adults aged 18 to 64 get at least 150 minutes of moderate-intensity aerobic activity each week. But here's the problem: less than half of us actually meet this bar. Can you guess the number-one reason we give? It's 'I don't have the time'! What's fascinating is that the very thing we don't have time for can be the key to prolonging the amount of time we have. A study revealed that the more time you spend sitting, the higher your risk of early death. They found:

- participants who sat for more than 13 hours per day had a 200 per cent greater risk of death than those who sat for less than 11 hours
- those who sat for shorter durations (less than 30 minutes at a time) had a 55 per cent lower risk of early death than those who sat for 30 minutes or more at a time
- individuals who frequently sat for longer than 90 minutes at a time were approximately twice as likely to die early than those who consistently limited their sitting time to less than 90 minutes.

It sounds to me like we have to spend time if we want to make time.

Two minutes is better than no minutes

Let's go back to the all-or-something mindset now and think about relaxing our internal guidelines for time and exercise – let's think about two minutes to begin with. How much more achievable does two minutes sound compared to 30 minutes or 60 minutes? So much more! But you might be thinking, *Two minutes? What's that going to do? Can that even make a difference?* Well, research suggests it can.

An exciting study led by the University of Sydney's Charles Perkins Centre has revealed the significant health benefits of vigorous intermittent lifestyle physical activity (VILPA). VILPA refers to short bursts of intense activity, lasting up to one to two minutes, that we engage in during our daily tasks, such as power walking when you're late to a meeting or running for the bus. The study found that the presence of just three or four one-minute bouts of VILPA in our daily routines is associated with remarkable reductions in the risk of premature death, especially from cardiovascular disease. The results show a reduction of up to 40 per cent in all-cause and cancer-related mortality, along with a staggering 49 per cent reduction in death related to cardiovascular disease. A different study found that even a single two-minute burst of high-intensity exercise a day, which comes to just 14 minutes a week, was associated with an impressive 18 per cent reduction in the risk of all-cause mortality. In other words, incorporating just a few minutes of vigorous activity into one's routine can have a substantial impact on longevity.

The evidence doesn't stop there. A Harvard Medical School study involving more than 5600 women over a five-year period found that reducing sedentary time by one hour a day was associated with a 26 per cent reduction in the risk of heart disease. And guess what? This hour didn't have to be consecutive; the effect could be achieved through short, light-intensity interruptions to sitting. Additionally, a study at Columbia University revealed that even just one minute of walking after every 30 minutes of sitting led to significant decreases in fatigue and significant improvements in mood. Lastly, if even just two minutes feels too hard some days, I still have good news for you: according to a study from Edith Cowan University, lifting weights for as little as three seconds a day can positively impact muscle strength. Yes, you read that right: three *tiny* seconds!

The two-minute trick

The next time you hear yourself say you don't have the time to exercise, try the two-minute trick. Tell yourself, *I'm just going to do two minutes.* If you keep going after the two minutes is up, that's great. If you don't, that's fine too. The research is clear that you'll still get incredible benefits from that moment of movement – and remember, all those little moments start to add up. See for yourself when you try out the micro moves in upcoming chapters.

Here are some other ideas to bust the excuse of having no time:

- Commit to doing angled push-ups at the kitchen bench when waiting for water to boil.
- Stand and pace when on the phone.
- Do a few heel raises when waiting for photocopying or printing.

Excuse buster 4: accept that active breaks are productive and necessary

Stopping work to prioritise your wellbeing can feel like an unwelcome interruption, a detour from your race to success. The inclination to defer self-care creeps in – maybe later, tomorrow or at some undefined time in the future. After all, the immediate focus is on pushing forward to conquer the tasks ahead.

A different, strategic perspective

My family's obsession with the Netflix series *Formula 1: Drive to Survive* has pulled me into a world I never anticipated being the least bit interested in: Formula One racing. Watching the high-stakes races, witnessing the speed, precision and unwavering determination of the drivers, I found myself drawing parallels to our own work lives and stumbled upon an intriguing perspective that might shift the way you think about taking a quick active break.

Imagine a Formula One driver in the heat of a race. They're intensely focused on maintaining their speed, navigating turns and overtaking competitors. It's a relentless pursuit of victory – much like our own daily endeavours. Just like those drivers, we're all racing towards our own finish lines, chasing after success and tenaciously tackling the challenges that come our way. In Formula One, where victory can be determined by mere milliseconds, the importance of pit stops is evident. Pit stops aren't disruptions or inconveniences; they're strategic moves that are essential for success. The crew refuels and fine-tunes the car, and changes its tyres – all necessary actions to maintain its peak performance. Similarly, as we navigate the race of productivity, our pit stops take the form of moments of movement – essential, purposeful breaks that reinvigorate us.

At first glance, these micro moves might appear inconsequential, almost counterproductive. After all, who wants to halt their momentum when the finish line is in sight? However, the key is recognising their significance – these short breaks are the very essence of wellbeing and productivity. They may last mere seconds or extend to a few minutes, yet their impact is profound.

Pit stops in your daily race

Imagine each moment of movement is a personal pit stop in your daily race – a moment to stretch, take a deep breath and reset. Picture movement itself as being akin to the work of a pit crew fine-tuning a car, ensuring it's optimised for the track ahead. By embracing moments of movement you're refuelling your energy, reigniting your focus and making necessary tweaks to maintain your performance.

In the world of Formula One, track conditions can change swiftly, prompting teams to adapt by changing tires or altering their strategy. Similarly, our workdays are rife with changing circumstances. Moments of movement offer the opportunity to recalibrate, evaluate and adjust our approach to new challenges. They grant us the perspective needed to re-evaluate priorities, tweak strategies and stay on course.

Embracing moments of movement is akin to a Formula One driver recognising the right time for a pit stop. It's about understanding that a brief pause for rejuvenation actually fuels your ability to sustain speed and focus throughout the race. These moments of renewal aren't distractions. Rather, they're key to maintaining peak performance, sidestepping burnout and crossing the day's finish line with renewed energy and enthusiasm. Sometimes a few seconds is all it takes to get your 'vehicle' back on track.

Excuse buster 5: no one needs to know

By now you might be thinking: *Hold on, I can't drop and do fifty push-ups in my office – what would people think?* Don't worry. I'm not asking you to do a full cardio class next to your computer. I promise you, a lot of the moves you'll discover in coming chapters are so subtle that your co-workers may not even notice you're doing them. (Even if they do, you're being a really great role model, and I hope they join in!) In the meantime, here is sneak peek of what's ahead.

TRY THIS: undercover chairercise

Sometimes you need to be a master of disguise to fit physical activity into your workday. Getting up for a series of star jumps when you're in the middle of a long, serious virtual meeting or surrounded by colleagues in the office might not be for you. That's where undercover chairercise – the ultimate sneaky and discreet energiser break that won't raise any eyebrows – comes in. These undercover chairercise moves are your secret allies in keeping your body engaged and refreshed right under everyone's nose.

The 'I've dropped my pen' reach-down

The 'I've dropped my pen' reach-down is a dynamic move that provides a gentle lower-back stretch while activating your core muscles, helping you maintain a strong and stable posture. Pay attention to your body's sensations and ensure that the movement remains comfortable and within your range of motion.

1. Imagine a case full of pens has dropped on the floor by each side of your feet and you need to pick them all up.
2. With a fluid and purposeful motion, reach down towards the floor next to your left foot with your left hand as if you're reaching for the pens. Feel the gentle stretch along the right side of your body and engage your core muscles to support the movement.
3. Return to an upright position, maintaining excellent posture and alignment.
4. Repeat the movement with your right hand, reaching towards your right foot as if you're reaching for another pen. Engage your core muscles and focus on the gentle stretch along your left side.
5. Perform several repetitions on each side, gradually increasing the fluidity and range of the reach while maintaining control and stability.

The 'look behind' twist

This movement adds a twist – literally – to your undercover chairercise routine. It's designed to gently work your core and back muscles while offering a moment of rejuvenation.

1. Begin by sitting up tall in your chair with your feet flat on the floor and your hands resting on your thighs.
2. Slowly twist your upper body to the right, crossing your left hand in front of you to rest on your right thigh. Gaze over your right shoulder.
3. Hold this twist for a few seconds, feeling the gentle stretch along your back and neck.
4. Release the twist and gently return to the centre.
5. Repeat the twist to the left side, crossing your right hand in front of you to rest on your left thigh. Gaze over your left shoulder.
6. Perform several repetitions on each side, enjoying the gentle stretch and revitalising sensation.

The 'tying my shoelace' move

Craving an undercover stretch for your lower body? Pretend you're subtly adjusting your shoe or tying up your shoelace with this subtle move that treats your hamstrings and hip flexors to a well-deserved stretch.

1. Start by sitting up straight in your chair, your feet resting comfortably on the floor.
2. Extend your left leg forward and flex your left foot, pointing your toes upward – the classic shoelace-tying pose.
3. Gently lean forward from your hips as if you're reaching for your laces or the tips of your toes.
4. Feel that delightful lengthening along the back of your left leg – the stretch in your hamstring. Hang out in this moment and relish the sensation.
5. Back to the upright position you go, sitting tall and proud.

6. Now, it's time to share the love with your right leg. Extend it forward, flex your foot and lean in for the undercover stretch, treating your right hamstring and hip flexors to their moment in the spotlight.

Excuse busted! In the second part of this book – 'Redesign: The active workday toolkit' – you'll discover a wealth of micro moves to help you overcome various other roadblocks.

Core points

- When you embark on your active workday journey, it's perfectly normal to face roadblocks. How can you see these as opportunities for a mindset makeover?
- How can you focus on what you can do, rather than on the limitations in your life, such as the amount of time you have to exercise or the current limitations of your physical body?
- Is an all-or-nothing mindset holding you back? Put aside any preconceived ideas of what 'exercise' looks like to explore the full spectrum of how it could look and feel for you.
- Try swapping the word 'exercise' for 'energise' and see how it feels and impacts your motivation.
- Remember, two minutes is better than no minutes, so get curious about ways you can add two minutes of movement to your workday today. Trust me, this is just the start of a new way to work – and to feel.

3

Don't wait for motivation

Take action now

A body at rest will remain at rest, and a body in motion will remain in motion, unless it is acted upon by an external force.

Isaac Newton

'I can't find the motivation.'

We've all said those words (or similar), felt that inertia and battled against the seemingly insurmountable wall that stands between us and exercise. Though we know we need to be active, motivation eludes us. The inner dialogue becomes a tug of war between intention and resistance that prevents us from taking action. We wait for motivation to strike, and as we wait we do nothing. But here's the thing: it's the taking of action that gives us motivation, not the other way around. Action precedes motivation.

The momentum of action

I remember the exact moment I discovered just how powerful this idea of action before motivation could be. A few months after doing that first plié at my kitchen bench, my daughter Stella (a toddler at the time) said, 'Let's have a dance, Mum!' Normally, because of my mental state at the time, I'd have made up some excuse for why I couldn't, but this time I said yes.

I put Stella on one hip and my baby Ruby on the other and started dancing. I'll never forget looking each of them right in their eyes as we danced. It felt like the first time I had really seen them for so long. I felt this energy and joy that I'd forgotten I could access. The first plié I did at my kitchen bench, which felt so hard and that I'd had no motivation to do, made the next day of movement that little bit easier. Slowly, these pliés opened me up to more daily movement and allowed me to take another step: dancing with the two most precious little people in my life.

There's a powerful principle that explains why two minutes of movement and exercise is better than none and why even a few seconds can make a difference: it's the notion that action precedes motivation. When we get active with even the tiniest step, we set off a cycle that propels us forward. Each action builds momentum, making it increasingly easy to continue and progress.

We often find ourselves waiting for the perfect conditions or for motivation to strike before engaging in any form of exercise. We find ourselves thinking that we need a significant chunk of time, ample energy or the ideal circumstances to kickstart our active journey. However, this tends to keep us stuck in a loop of inaction and waiting. By shifting our mindset and embracing the principle that action precedes motivation, we liberate ourselves from needing external factors to align perfectly. Instead, we recognise that taking even the smallest step, such as a few seconds of movement, can set the wheels in motion. It creates a positive feedback loop that fuels our motivation and desire to continue.

When we start moving, we feel our blood flowing, our muscles awakening and our breath deepening. These sensations are powerful triggers that ignite a desire for more. They remind us of the inherent joy and vitality that movement brings. Furthermore, each action we take, regardless of duration or intensity, builds upon the previous action. It can strengthen our resolve, boost our self-esteem and reinforce a positive association with exercise. As we accumulate these small victories, we develop an internal drive that propels us to seek more opportunities for movement.

The momentum of action transforms our health and wellbeing and can also permeate other aspects of our lives. As we witness our ability to follow through on commitments and overcome inertia, we cultivate a mindset of resilience and discipline. This mindset spills over into other domains, empowering us to tackle challenges, pursue goals and make positive changes.

It's like a stationary steam train. The effort to get that thing moving is enormous, but little by little it becomes easier, momentum builds and it's on its way. Embrace the power of those tiny moments that lead you to your future self. Don't underestimate them. Trust in their ability to make a remarkable difference in your life. These small actions create a ripple effect that might stretch beyond what you can imagine.

Relying on motivation can be precarious because it can be so inconsistent. Motivation is far from constant, surging one day and disappearing the next, potentially damaging progress and causing procrastination when it wanes. Relying on motivation is like relying on a gust of wind: it can propel you forward briefly, if it comes along at all, but you need a sturdy sail and a steady hand to be sure of getting to where you want to go. We need to have some much more reliable strategies up our sleeves. Let's dive into four of them.

Shift your perspective

Resistance, that tough opponent, surfaces especially when we stand on the precipice of something significant. In *The War of Art*, Steven Pressfield captures this concept beautifully. He describes resistance as a formidable force we encounter when we feel a strong aversion towards doing something. But Pressfield challenges us to view resistance in a new light. Rather than being a sign that we should turn away, resistance signals tasks with the greatest meaning and purpose.

When we experience resistance towards physical activity – the groans, the excuses, the reluctance – it's actually a clue that we're on the right track. It's a signal that we're venturing into territory that holds value for us. The greater the resistance to doing something, the more likely it is that we need to do it. Resistance is our minds communicating that the task has the potential to change us, enhancing our wellbeing, boosting our energy and elevating our quality of life. So, stop feeling guilty for your lack of motivation and start to see it as a good thing – you're moving in the right direction.

Rather than perceiving resistance as an insurmountable obstacle, try shifting your perspective to see it as a positive force propelling you towards an active workday. The more resistance you encounter, the more certain you can be that the endeavour holds meaning. Resistance serves as a litmus test for the significance of your actions.

TRY THIS: befriending resistance

Pause and reflect on a time when you resisted doing something you knew would benefit you, such as exercsing. Close your eyes if it helps you focus. Envision the resistance you experienced as a character standing before you. What does this character look like? Give them a name, perhaps 'Mr Resistance' or 'Ms Doubt'.

After taking a deep breath, greet your resistance character with a friendly smile. Ask them, 'Why are you here? What are you trying to protect me from?' Listen attentively to what your resistance character has to say. They might express fears, doubts or opinions that have been holding you back from getting active. They might say things like, 'You're too busy to exercise', or, 'It's too hard'. Now, imagine gently patting your resistance character on the back, saying, 'Thanks for wanting to keep me safe and comfortable, but I'm going to do it anyway!'

Open your eyes now and reflect on this exercise and your emotions. Recognise that resistance is a natural facet of growth. By acknowledging it and playfully engaging with it, you can relegate the voice of resistance to the passenger seat instead of letting it steer.

In the wise words of Elizabeth Gilbert in *Big Magic: Creative living beyond fear*, fear 'doesn't get to hold the map. It doesn't get to choose the snacks. It doesn't get to ever suggest detours'. It's time to regain control from resistance, because moving your body puts you at a genuine advantage.

Accountability is your co-pilot

In conquering motivational obstacles, accountability is your steadfast ally. It adds a layer of commitment beyond your own intentions.

Picture this scenario: it's almost noon and you've made a promise to yourself to take a quick walk during your lunch break. You know it's good for your wellbeing and you genuinely want to incorporate more movement into your day. However, as the clock strikes 12, your overflowing inbox and mounting tasks overshadow your initial enthusiasm. You find yourself debating whether to skip the walk just this once.

Sound familiar? We've all been there, witness to the clash between our best intentions and our daily responsibilities. It's easy to tell ourselves that we'll make up for it later or go for a walk tomorrow when things are less hectic.

Let's add a twist now. Imagine the same situation: the same pressing workload and the same temptation to skip the walk. This time, however, you've committed to meet a colleague outside for that lunchtime walk. This changes things. The idea of cancelling or postponing becomes less enticing. You know your colleague is waiting and you've made a pact to prioritise an active workday. Despite the to-do list and emails beckoning from your desk, the thought of breaking your commitment and letting your colleague down compels you to get up, put on your sneakers and step outside.

What happened here? Accountability entered the picture. The mere presence of a commitment transformed your approach. It's no longer just about you and your intentions; it's about honouring your promise to another person. This shift in perspective indicates a powerful truth: accountability can be the driving force that turns intentions into actions, even in the face of distractions and competing priorities.

This shows that accountability can be a game-changer – the nudge that propels you forward, the reminder that keeps you on track and the supportive hand that helps you overcome resistance. Integrating accountability into your pursuit of an active workday means you're no longer navigating the journey alone. You're part of a team, a partnership that empowers you to rise above challenges and embrace the benefits of movement.

Here are five ideas for how you can bring accountability into your active workday:

1. **Enlist an accountability buddy.** Find someone who shares your commitment to an active workday. Having someone to check in and share your progress with can be incredibly motivating. It becomes a shared journey in which you can encourage each other, celebrate achievements and offer support during challenging times.
2. **Tap into accountability apps.** Use apps that send you reminders or notifications to move throughout the day. Some apps even allow you to connect with others striving for an active lifestyle.
3. **Create a movement challenge.** Set up a friendly competition or challenge within your team or with friends. This could involve tracking steps, active minutes or any other form of movement. A shared goal and a bit of healthy competition can inspire everyone to stay active and engaged.
4. **Buddy up for moving meetings.** Pair up with a colleague for movement-focused meetings. Instead of sitting down for discussions, walk together while you talk. This fosters a dynamic environment for brainstorming and problem-solving.
5. **Make a public commitment.** Share your commitment to an active workday publicly with your team or network. This could be through company-wide communication, an internal platform

or even a social media post. By making your intentions known you invite accountability and support from your colleagues and friends.

Remember, accountability isn't about adding pressure; rather, it's about creating a supportive network that helps you stay on track and celebrate successes. As you explore these strategies and incorporate accountability into your active workday journey, you'll find that the collective effort enhances your wellbeing and the overall culture at your workplace (more on that in part III).

Confronting the challenge of exercising and depression

In an article published on the Harvard Health Publishing blog, Assistant Professor of Psychiatry at Harvard Medical School Dr Michael Craig Miller reaches a remarkable conclusion: exercise can be as effective as medication in treating some cases of depression, offering the added benefit of fewer side effects. (Please note, my intention in including this study is to highlight the power of exercise, not to minimise the effectiveness of medication.) This endorsement echoes the recommendations of doctors, mental health experts and the World Health Organization, who advocate for exercise as a potent remedy for enhancing mental wellbeing. The profound impact of exercise on our emotions and mental state is supported by science, and it's an essential tool in the battle against depression.

However, there's a significant hurdle to overcome. Finding the motivation and energy to engage in physical activity feels challenging when you're experiencing depression – or even just feeling a bit down. The lethargy and lack of interest that often accompany low mood can create a vicious cycle, stopping us from initiating the very activity that could bring relief.

Negative self-perception and self-doubt may further impede progress, leading us to believe we lack the capability or that exercise won't be helpful. Moreover, depression can diminish our ability to experience pleasure, making the thought of participating in activities that once brought joy seem unappealing or futile. Before I experienced depression, if I heard about someone struggling with their mental health I would think, *You just need to exercise!* But I quickly discovered that it wasn't that simple. Here's a different approach that worked for me and I've found works for a lot of people.

Start really, really small

When I was struggling with postnatal depression, just two minutes of exercise a day was a game-changer (and ended up inspiring a global movement). I started out with the primary goal of introducing short bursts of movement – first into my own daily routine and then into other people's – to infuse challenging days with some happiness, strength and joy.

When confronting low mood or depression, small moments of movement offer a gentle and practical approach to kickstarting your journey towards improved mental wellbeing. That could look like getting up from your desk, stretching your arms up for a moment and sitting back down, or even doing a couple of push-ups at the kitchen bench when making a cup of tea. The brevity ensures you can engage in them without feeling overwhelmed or discouraged, giving you a foundation from which to build momentum over time.

As you engage in movement and experience the positive impact on your mood, self-esteem and overall wellbeing, you'll begin to feel more confident in your ability to incorporate movement into your life, empowering you over time to take on more physical activity in the future.

Be kind to yourself, celebrate every moment of progress and recognise that even the tiniest efforts towards movement are valuable investments in your mental health. Be sure to reach out and get support from health professionals, mental health organisations, support lines, and friends and family.

Discovering your 'why'

Why do you want to make changes to your sedentary workday? What significance does it hold for you when you choose to break up long hours of sitting with movement? Your 'why' assumes the role of a guiding North Star, propelling you towards a work life that's not only active but also deeply fulfilling.

TRY THIS: what's your 'why'?

Let's uncover your motivations and reveal your personal 'why' for embracing an active workday. This is the purpose behind your journey, and it will power and sustain your commitment to breaking up long hours of sitting with movement. Work through the following prompts to articulate your personal reasons for beginning – and continuing – this journey towards an a more active workday.

Make it personal

Take a moment to make your 'why' personal by defining your physical and mental fitness goals for integrating more movement into your workday. Is it about infusing your day with energy? Improving your mental clarity and focus? Having a less achy body? Enhancing your overall physical health?

Make it about your work life

Once these objectives are clear, delve deeper. Explore how these changes will shape your experience of the workday. How will they influence your work life, your career trajectory and the kind of professional you aspire to be, both within your workplace and beyond its confines? For example, 'With more energy I could put more effort into the work project I care about and make a real difference to my customers'.

Make it bigger than you

Contemplate the far-reaching consequences of your choice to lead an active workday. How will an energised and engaged version of you impact your relationships? How does this transformation resonate with your roles in life as a parent, partner, professional or friend? Consider how prioritising movement can enrich your connections, amplify your influence and inspire those around you. Ponder the interconnectedness between movement and your core values – whether it's setting an example for your family, being fully present in your interactions or nurturing your personal growth. Envision the narrative arc that your active workday will support.

Navigate using your 'why'

As you embark on a journey towards an active workday filled with energy and purpose, your 'why' serves as a compass, keeping you oriented towards your destination and steadfast in your commitment to get there. It will be a source of motivation during the inevitable challenges you'll encounter along the way. Each step becomes infused with meaning, every effort illuminated by your overarching purpose.

With your 'why' at the forefront of your mind, you're well-equipped to bridge the gap between your current work routine and the vibrant, active workday you aspire to. This journey isn't just about movement; it's about embracing a philosophy of vitality that extends beyond your workspace, impacting every facet of your life. Your 'why' propels you forward, turning a simple change into a transformative endeavour.

TRY THIS: visit your future self

Imagine yourself travelling forward in time five, ten, 20 or even more years. Picture yourself visiting someone of immense importance in your life. This person has guided you through challenges, celebrated your successes and imparted invaluable wisdom. This person is your future self. As you meet your future self, take a moment to observe, connect and reflect. How does your future self appear to you? What accomplishments are you proud of? What lessons have you learned? What habits did you cultivate that led you to this point?

Now, consider what actions you can take in the present to ensure your future self is the person you aspire to be. What choices will honour your future self's wellbeing, vitality and happiness? Use this exercise as a touchstone, a reminder of the incredible impact your choices today can have on the person you become tomorrow. By embracing an active workday, you're ensuring that your vision of your future self becomes a reality.

Core points

- There's a misconception that we need to wait to feel motivated to take action. In fact, action precedes motivation.
- When we experience resistance towards physical activity – the groans, the excuses, the reluctance – it's actually a clue that we're on the right track.
- The greater the resistance to doing something, the more likely it is that we need to do it.
- Return to the idea of befriending resistance; how can you talk back to your resistance and assure it that you're safe to move forward?
- When you get clear on your 'why', it helps you to stay on target. What is your very personal reason behind wanting to move more and how can you hold yourself accountable? This is key!

4

The path to lasting change

From willpower to sustainable habits

Habit will sustain you whether you're inspired or not.

Octavia E Butler

In the quest for a healthier work routine, integrating movement throughout the day is important. Yet, relying solely on sheer willpower to maintain this lifestyle shift can be a daunting and energy-draining endeavour. This is where cultivating sustainable habits comes into play. Why? Because habits hold the key to lasting success, consistency and transformative change.

Picture this: you wake up with determination, committed to breaking up the long hours of sitting in the workday ahead. You start strongly, but as the day progresses your energy wanes and so does your willpower. By the afternoon, your seat becomes harder to break away from and your initial enthusiasm falters. This scenario isn't uncommon, as willpower is a finite resource that depletes over time – and that's why it's not enough to rely on.

Habits, on the other hand, operate differently. They're your brain's autopilot, executing actions with minimal effort or conscious thought. Habits require less energy to maintain than willpower. Once an action becomes habitual, it's woven into the fabric of your daily routine, making it a natural and almost effortless part of your life.

When you first started driving, for example, the individual actions involved in safely performing that complex task demanded your focused attention. You had to concentrate on every little thing, from remembering to indicate and check your mirrors to following traffic rules. However, as you gained experience, these individual actions required less mental effort. Now you might even arrive at your destination without fully recalling the drive itself.

Similarly, making moments of movement in your work routine habitual can mean that the moves don't demand much mental effort at all. You might even find yourself doing them automatically. By transforming the individual elements of an active workday into habits, you eliminate the mental tug-of-war between wanting to move and the comfort of remaining sedentary. Habits bypass the need for constant motivation or decision-making, making it easier to leave inertia behind. This shift from relying on willpower to embracing habits frees up mental energy for other tasks and decisions, ultimately reducing decision fatigue.

But how do we form habits? It's all about the power of three: a cue, an action and a reward. The cue triggers the action and the reward reinforces it, making the routine more likely to become a habit. In this chapter I break down each element of this cue-action-reward habit loop to help you gather momentum and create lasting change.

1. The cue: finding the prompt

The first element of habit formation is the cue – the ignition switch that kickstarts the desired behaviour. Think of it as something that prompts you to act. Identifying and using effective cues is crucial in building habits that stand the test of time.

The potency of cues lies in the strength of their link to the desired action in your mind. Over time, this association becomes stronger, making the behaviour more automatic. Imagine your cues as friendly nudges guiding you towards the actions you want to take.

Your workflow: harnessing the power of habit stacking

One effective technique for integrating movement into your workday is known as 'habit stacking'. This involves 'stacking' a new behaviour onto an existing behaviour, creating a smoother path for adopting and maintaining it as a habit. This method, popularised by BJ Fogg as part of his Tiny Habits program, can be used to turn everyday actions into obvious cues to help you form nearly any habit.

You already have many established activities during your workday: sending emails, attending meetings, making phone calls and taking short breaks to get some water or go to the bathroom, for example. Using Fogg's habit-stacking framework, these everyday tasks serve as your 'anchors'. You can then pair that anchor with an active moment to create a new, beneficial habit that sits seamlessly within your workflow. The pairing process might unfold like this:

Before I [insert anchor task], I will [insert movement].

When I [insert anchor task], I will [insert movement].

After I [insert anchor task], I will [insert movement].

Anchors act as prompts for your new habits. Over time your mind associates these regular activities with the subsequent movements, making them a natural and integral part of your daily workflow. Here are some ideas for workflow habit stacking:

- Before I join a virtual meeting, I will turn my head from side to side to relax my neck muscles.
- When I take a sip of water, I will stand up and stretch.
- After I send an email, I will stretch my arms up to the ceiling and take a big, deep breath.
- Before I open a new document, I will roll my shoulders forwards and backwards.
- When I pick up the phone, I will stand and do ten heel raises.
- After I flick on the kettle, I will do ten angled push-ups at the kitchen counter while waiting for the water to boil.

As I'll explain in a moment, the key to successful habit stacking is consistency. Be intentional about executing these actions regularly until they become automatic. Set reminders or create visual cues to reinforce the behaviour until it becomes second nature.

Visit lizziewilliamson.com/active to download a list of ideas for workflow habit stacking. This is great for printing out and sticking above your desk or in a communal workspace.

TRY THIS: take a mental snapshot

No one knows the ins and outs of your workday as you do, so picture the tasks, routines and procedures that fill your hours. When you look at this mental snapshot, one or two recurring activities are likely to stand out. It could be the numerous emails you send, the phone calls you make or the virtual meetings you attend. These activities present perfect opportunities to introduce movement cues.

Choose one task that you do every day. This is the anchor to which you can attach your new habit – a simple practice that infuses a touch of activity into your routine. Envision how you can seamlessly incorporate a moment of movement before, during or after this chosen task – you'll have plenty of ideas after reading the second part of this book. Allow this task to prompt you to take a quick break from your static work and introduce a refreshing burst of physical motion. As you consistently respond to this cue, it naturally becomes a habit that nurtures your physical wellbeing and enhances your overall experience at work.

Use digital cues: anchoring movement in your routine

> *'Every day at 10 a.m., my calendar gives me this message: "One-minute break". At first, those one-minute breaks were no big deal – just a quick stretch or a short walk outside, you know? But I stuck with them like clockwork because I knew I was sitting way too much. Rain or shine, even when work was nuts, that 10 a.m. ping turned into something sacred. And you know*

what? Those tiny moments started changing up my whole work scene.' – Joe

In the flow of work, it's easy to lose track of time and unintentionally stay glued to our seats for prolonged periods. The result? A stiff body and a weary brain. Fortunately, technology can be a valuable ally to free us from this trap.

Digital cues act as virtual companions, prodding you to shift your focus from the screen to your body's wellbeing. Here are four digital cues to keep your active workday on track:

1. **Screen break alarms.** Set a recurring alarm on your computer or phone for those times in the day you usually sit for hours without taking a break. When the alarm sounds, pause for a minute to stretch, stand up or take a short stroll around your workspace. If you use your phone for this, put it out of reach so you have to actually get up to silence the alarm!

   Example: Every day at 11 a.m. my phone alarm reminds me to stand and stretch.

2. **Meeting transition prompts.** Use your calendar app to set reminders before virtual meetings. Use this opportunity to stand, move or do a quick stretch.

   Example: At the five-minute reminder before each meeting, I'll do a one-minute walk around to get my creative juices flowing.

3. **Hourly phone chimes.** Set an hourly or half-hourly chime on your phone to remind you to shift positions or do a quick movement routine. Again, place your phone slightly out of reach so you have to get up to turn off the reminder.

   Example: Every hour, I'll take a two-minute walk when my phone chimes.

4. **Digital sticky notes.** Place virtual sticky notes on your screen as visual cues to move. Seeing these notes reminds you to incorporate movement breaks.

   Example: Reminder – stretch your legs!

Your body and brain: tuning into your wellbeing radar

> *'I like that the awareness to move, even just a little bit, seems to be a daily thing now. I find myself stretching more, wiggling my hips, just having more awareness in general. It doesn't mean I always follow my own advice, but at least I notice and then choose to act.' – Nick*

What if we became more attuned to the subtle signals our bodies and minds send us? Imagine using these signals – the minor discomforts, the restlessness, the moments of feeling less productive – as cues that prompt you to move.

Think of these cues as your wellbeing radar, finely tuned to detect the shifts within you. When you feel a niggle in your body – perhaps a tense shoulder or a stiff neck – it's your cue that you need a burst of movement. When your mind drifts and your productivity wanes, it's your cue to reset and engage in a micro move. These whispers from within, which you may have been ignoring for years now, are gently reminding you to attend to your wellbeing.

This practice of listening to your body and mind is akin to learning a new melody. At first, you might need to pay close attention to the notes, ensuring you catch every nuance. As you respond to your body's cues, you create a rhythm – a natural ebb and flow between focused work and refreshing moves.

Over time, these cues become familiar companions. Your body's niggles become friendly reminders, gently nudging you towards self-care through movement. The dips in productivity become cues for action rather than sources of frustration. This practice becomes woven into the fabric of your workday – a melody that you can play without missing a beat:

- When my lower back starts to ache, I will do a gentle twist from side to side.
- After I notice shoulder tightness, I will roll my shoulders back five times.

- When I start to get distracted, I will roll down towards my toes, take a deep breath and roll back up.
- After I yawn, I will get up for a quick walk on the spot.

Remember, just as a musician practises until playing an instrument becomes second nature, embracing movement cues takes practice too. With each cue you respond to, you reinforce the connection between these triggers and movement, and prioritise your wellbeing.

2. The action: your routine

You've set the stage by creating cues that nudge you to incorporate more movement into your workday. Now it's time to bring those intentions to life. Welcome to the 'routine' phase of the habit loop, where you put your plans into action. This is your opportunity to put on your metaphorical sneakers, roll up your sleeves and get moving. In the words of John C Maxwell, 'You'll never change your life until you change something you do daily. The secret of your success is found in your daily routine'.

When choosing your routine or action, follow the pillars of ACT – achievable, consistent and tailored – to set yourself up for success.

Achievable: embracing the philosophy of small and steady progress

'Like many people, my workday is extremely busy. I set myself a goal to stand up every 30 minutes, but every time my alarm went off, I ignored it. Then Lizzie suggested that I make my goal even simpler and focus on one achievable action a day. So, I set myself the goal of taking one "mini walk" for two minutes during my first phone call of the day – and it worked! Now, it's just part of me. If I'm on a call and don't need to jot down notes, I stand without even thinking. It's crazy how weird it feels to sit while talking now. Seriously, who would've thought? But here I am!' – Clare

Why focus on achievability? Simply put, when an action is achievable, the likelihood of consistent execution increases exponentially. Achievability is the gateway to consistency and, ultimately, the transformation of actions into habits.

If you want to feel and be stronger but getting down on the floor for 50 push-ups in your workday doesn't feel achievable to you, think about what does. How about five angled push-ups with your hands on the wall or kitchen counter? Trust in the small steps to get you going.

Consistent: keeping the pulse of progress

> *'Confession time: I wasn't sure those quick stand-up breaks between meetings would do much. I mean, how could a few seconds really matter? Still, I decided to stick with them through a year of non-stop meetings. And now, looking back, it's undeniable that they've made a difference. My energy levels are way steadier. And that end-of-day burnout? Not nearly as bad.' – Jarrod*

Why is consistency such a crucial player in this game of change? Think of it like learning to play a musical instrument. At first, it's a struggle. You forget to practise for a few days and return to square one at your next attempt. But then you commit to daily practice, even if it's just for a short time. What happens? Slowly but surely, your fingers become accustomed to the keys, frets, valves or strings, the cadences become familiar and the melody takes shape. It's not about hours of practice in one go; it's about the repetition, the steady pulse of progress that brings mastery. Consistency is the magic of habits.

The key to long-term success is achievability. So, start super small, and if you're still struggling to keep it up, go even smaller. If you're finding it hard to consistently do five push-ups each day, do one. Remember, a couple of seconds is better than no seconds!

Tailored: personalising your path to activity

> *'I am disabled (lots of back pain when standing and moving), but I need exercise really badly! I've discovered that one or two minutes is the perfect length to get me out of breath and feeling*

the effort. I then take a ten-minute break to let my back rest and then I do it again!' – Fran

In the world of movement, there's no one-size-fits-all approach. Just as a perfectly tailored outfit enhances your style and comfort, customising your movement routine to your unique needs elevates your wellbeing. Your journey to an active workday is as personal as your fingerprint, and finding movement choices that resonate with you is important.

Creating your own movement blueprint is part of this. Are you starting from scratch or looking to refine an existing routine? The beauty of this journey is that it's entirely yours and it begins by assessing where you stand. If you're not feeling at your peak fitness level, don't worry. Start with activities that don't intimidate you. Gentle stretching, leisurely walking or even a brief chair yoga session can be excellent starting points. Remember, the aim is to create a positive association with movement, not to immediately push yourself to your limit. Here are my tips for creating your movement blueprint:

- **Adapt to your body.** Consider your body's uniqueness. Are there any physical limitations or injuries that require special attention? Listen to your body's signals and find alternative movements that cater to your situation. Movement should nurture, not harm. You can ensure a sustainable and safe journey towards an active workday by respecting your body's boundaries.
- **Stay in your comfort zone.** Comfort plays a pivotal role in embracing an active workday. If you're uncomfortable moving around in front of others, there's no pressure to do so. Opt for movements you can seamlessly incorporate into your workday without drawing attention. Alternatively, find a quiet corner for gentle stretches or quick exercises. On the flip side, if you thrive on movement and enjoy being active, let your enthusiasm guide you. Dance, walk or stretch to your heart's content!
- **Be flexible in your routine.** Life is a tapestry of changing circumstances; your movement routine should flow with it.

Some days, you might find unexpected tasks stacking up, leaving less time for your usual walk. On such occasions, accepting flexibility in your routine is essential. Embrace quick desk stretches or stand-up exercises that can fit around your workload. Make movement part of your day, no matter the form it takes.

- **Choose movement that suits you.** Each day brings its own energy, challenges and commitments. The key to success is tailoring your movement to suit. Whether you do a set of squats or a few minutes of stretching, your moments of movement are uniquely yours. The goal is to make physical activity an effortless part of your routine, something that enhances your wellbeing without causing stress.

Just as you can't lift weights once and expect a transformation, change comes from sustained effort. It's not the single bicep curl that shapes your body but the repetitions performed consistently over time. Similarly, adopting consistent behaviours, no matter how minor, gradually reshapes your routine and, ultimately, your life.

3. The reward: sealing the habit loop

Rewards keep us coming back for more, and they're scattered throughout our daily lives. Ever felt a rush when your phone pings with a message, or the sense of accomplishment when you complete a task? These feelings silently nudge us towards forming habits, whether we're aware of it or not.

Rewards play a pivotal role in habit formation by targeting the brain's pleasure centre. This centre is fuelled by the release of neurotransmitters such as dopamine and endorphins – chemicals associated with feelings of pleasure, satisfaction and wellbeing.

This is why rewards are pivotal in sealing the habit loop and cementing those behaviours – your brain learns to associate the action with a sense of accomplishment and joy. As habit guru BJ Fogg writes, 'There is a direct connection between what you feel when you do a behaviour and the likelihood that you will repeat the behaviour in the future'. Social media companies know all about the reward system of the brain. The pings, dings and hearts we receive when using their platforms trigger the release of dopamine, keeping us returning for more and more.

Now let's delve into the multifaceted nature of rewards. These rewards encompass both intrinsic and bodily rewards, the satisfaction of ticking off a goal on a habit tracker and the meaningful yet simple act of celebration.

The inherent rewards of movement: finding joy in every step

The beauty of movement lies in the rewards inherent in each action. Consider how you feel after a satisfying stretch: having lengthened your muscles and taken a moment to breathe deeply, on releasing the stretch you're met with a sensation of rejuvenation. It's as if your body is whispering its gratitude for the care you've shown it. This feeling then becomes a compelling incentive to repeat that stretch whenever you need a boost.

Think about the brisk walk that clears your mind like a breath of fresh air. As you step outdoors and feel the rhythm of your feet hitting the ground, your thoughts begin to align and clarity emerges from the mental fog. The experience of sheer mental liberation becomes a reward that beckons you to lace up your shoes and step out again and again.

These experiences, simple yet deeply transformative, can become your new norm – and something you look forward to. The reward isn't some distant outcome; it's nestled within the very act of moving. Vitality surges through your veins, a calmness settles over your mind and a sense of accomplishment descends gently.

Achieving goals: unlocking your inner motivator with activity trackers

Tracking your activity on your smartwatch or phone with any of the free apps available offers you a visual record of your progress and lets you see how far you've come. It also allows you to set achieve activity goals and then helps you achieve them. Whether it's the satisfying closure of your activity ring on your smartwatch or the cheerful ding when you hit your step goal, the sense of accomplishment that they trigger drives you forward. They are your own personal motivators.

Setting goals is part of being human and tracking takes this innate desire to a new level. When you set targets for steps, active minutes or movement breaks, you're essentially drawing a map for a more active workday. These goals become checkpoints, guiding you towards accomplishments and highlighting how far you've come. It's where the magic happens – achieving a goal releases dopamine, a feel-good neurotransmitter. This biochemical reaction links movement with pleasure, making you want to chase those goals even more so you can bask in the satisfaction of accomplishment.

This makes activity tracking a stealthy tool for forming lasting habits. By consistently carrying out (and then recording) an activity, you're carving a groove in your brain. Over time, that groove becomes a habit. So, as you log your movement day after day and feel that satisfaction, you're teaching your brain that being active leads to feeling awesome. With practice, this connection becomes second nature. You won't even have to think about it; it'll simply be part of your daily routine.

My daughter Ruby loves the activity tracker on her watch so much that I asked for her thoughts on this section. This is what she said:

> *You know that feeling when you check something off your to-do list? Well, hitting my activity goals gives me that same kind of satisfaction. It's like I'm always moving forward, not going backward. It's funny because it kind of makes other tasks seem less daunting. Like, if I can take a walk, who's to say I can't clean my room?*

Celebration: the cherry on top

If you find movement challenging, or if your current physical situation means that movement isn't a rewarding experience, there's another way to access the reward system. Among the myriad rewards offered by exercise, celebration stands out as a remarkably effective, instant and accessible choice. Celebration taps into the core of human psychology, resonating deeply with our need for acknowledgment and positive reinforcement. When you celebrate your achievements, no matter how small, you're acknowledging your efforts and embracing your progress. This acknowledgment triggers a surge of positive emotions, closing the feedback loop that reinforces the behaviour you're trying to cultivate.

Making celebration a part of your habit loop is like installing a turbo boost for your positive actions. You're infusing those actions with positivity, reinforcing your commitment to change and creating a trail of pleasurable memories that your brain eagerly anticipates. Each time you celebrate, you're making it a little bit easier for your brain to say, 'Yes, let's do that again!' And the more you repeat this cycle, the stronger the habit becomes.

Celebrate the small victories and use them as a driving force for building your active workday habits. This is a powerful tool for reinforcing the third pillar of habit formation.

A fun, feel-good way to celebrate your victories and place that cherry on top of your brain's reward pathways is by having a moment of self-recognition in which you revel in the feeling of empowerment that comes from achieving what you set out to do. Imagine you've finished a marathon or just received some fantastic news. What physical action might you take? What positive affirmation might you say to yourself? Find an action or a phrase – or both! – that resonates with you and feels good, then commit to closing the habit loop with that action or phrase.

I call this a 'Woohoo, go you!' moment because that's what I say to myself. You might like to adopt this too, or you might prefer to adopt a different positive affirmation, such as a fist pump, happy dance, big smile, deep breath, mindful pause, shimmy or clap, or another excalamation, such as 'Yes!', 'Well done!' or 'You did it!'

In her book *The High 5 Habit*, motivational speaker Mel Robbins describes a simple yet powerful tool for changing her readers' attitudes, mindsets and behaviours: she encourages them to high-five themselves in the mirror, even if it feels confronting or strange to begin with. Since reading her book, I've made it a habit to high-five myself in the reflection of my computer, in the elevator mirror, in bathrooms, and even when I'm on screen for a virtual meeting before anyone has joined. These moments of celebrating my actions at work quieten that default critical voice trying to stop me from taking action again.

High fives are deeply ingrained – culturally and psychologically – as symbols of celebration and success. From sports victories to personal achievements, we associate high-fiving with moments of joy and positivity. When we use high fives to celebrate our actions and efforts, we leverage this built-in association to close a positive feedback loop in our brain.

Whenever you give yourself a high five after completing a micro move or engaging in an active behaviour, you tell your brain, 'This is a good thing. Let's do it again'. This boosts your motivation and strengthens the neural connections associated with that action. By consciously using the high-five gesture in a self-affirming and celebratory manner, you're capitalising on the positive emotions and reinforcement of the action. Your brain responds by releasing those feel-good neurotransmitters, making you more likely to repeat the action you're celebrating in the future.

Remember the link between high-fives and good feelings the next time you get active at work. Find your reflection somewhere, give yourself that high five and embrace the positivity and sense of achievement it brings. Your brain already knows the language of high fives – now it's time to let that language work in your favour as you establish the habits that will shape a more energetic, focused and productive work routine.

You can also use reward charts to close the habit loop. I had them for all sorts of things when my kids were little. I wanted to help them cultivate certain habits and behaviours, such as eating their vegetables, not biting one another or fighting and not getting out of bed a million times after I said goodnight. The positive action of celebrating each desired behaviour with a sticker on a chart and watching the stickers multiply worked wonders. For even more motivation, at the bottom of the chart would be a stated reward for a certain number of stickers.

The concept is so simple and effective, and its effectiveness isn't limited to kids – it's also handy for us adults, especially when we're building new habits. The magic of reward charts lies in their ability to tap into the joy of accomplishment. Think about the satisfaction of crossing items off your to-do list. The same principle applies here. Each sticker (or tick) becomes a badge of honour, a testament to your commitment to wellbeing. These small, celebratory acts amplify your sense of achievement, reinforcing positive behaviours and strengthening the neural pathways associated with movement.

You also have the option to establish a specific time period for the tracking progress. This time frame can provide structure and a sense of purpose. A weekly or monthly chart often works well, allowing you to see the immediate results of your efforts and providing frequent opportunities for rewards. For example, if you're trying to establish a daily micro move (more about micro moves in the second part of this book), a monthly chart can help you track your actions. At the end of the month or week, you can set a reward if you reach a certain number of ticks or stickers. This serves as an incentive to keep up positive habits and maintain consistency in your efforts, and it adds an extra layer of anticipation and accomplishment, encouraging you to reach your monthly target. Whether the reward is a special treat, something you've been waiting to buy or an experience, such as an afternoon at the gallery, it keeps you focused on your goals and reinforces the value of staying active throughout your workday.

TRY THIS: make a reward chart

Let's make a reward chart to get you started on your active workday habit-building journey. Download a copy from lizziewilliamson.com/active or follow these instructions to build your own:

1. First add a title to the top of the page (for example, 'Make a Move Reward Chart').

2. Next, draw a grid on a sheet of paper, making sure you have enough columns for a week's or month's worth of workdays.
3. At the top of each column, label the days of your work week or month. In the first row of each column, write down the specific action or goal you want to achieve to make your workday more active. It could be taking a two-minute stretch, going for a walk at lunch, using a stand-up desk for a specific time or taking the stairs instead of the elevator.
4. Determine the reward you'll give yourself and write it down at the bottom of the column.
5. Put up the chart near where you work. Find some stickers or a pen and reward yourself with a sticker or a tick on your chart every time you engage in a movement break or complete an active task. If another format would work better for you – perhaps a digital version on your device or even an app designed for habit tracking – you can use that instead.

As the days pass, your reward chart will blossom with evidence of your efforts, illustrating both your dedication and the power of consistency. Every tick, every sticker is a visual representation of your progress and a powerful reminder of the strides you're making towards a more active workday. Most importantly, just as with the other rewards I've described in this chapter, your brain will pick up on the pattern, and this visual representation of success will create a positive loop that encourages you to keep going.

Be kind to yourself as you build active workday habits

We aspire to make our habits achievable, consistent and tailored so they can be successful, but also to complete the habit loop by celebrating each small achievement. Nevertheless, it's important to acknowledge that amid our hectic workdays, unforeseen circumstances can see us fall off the active workday wagon. In these moments, it's crucial not to deem it all too hard and give up. Instead, these are opportune times to practise self-compassion and kindness.

You've probably heard that it takes 21 days to make a habit, but don't worry if it doesn't click that quickly for you. In fact, participants in one study needed anywhere from 18 to 254 days to lock in a habit. This shows that there is no magic amount of time and that we all have our own unique pace when embracing new behaviours. So, if a habit isn't sticking as fast as you'd hoped, you're in good company.

Everyone changes at their own pace. The journey from deliberate action to autopilot might take longer than you initially thought and that's perfectly okay. It might even happen quicker! It's all part of the journey. Consistency remains the special ingredient that eventually makes a habit feel as natural as breathing. Keep up the fantastic work, keep your actions achievable and know that each day you're getting closer to that sought-after autopilot mode. You're right on track.

Finally, missing a day here and there won't derail your progress. It's like skipping a note in a melody – you can still pick up the tune. Plus, remember how I discussed shifting from an all-or-nothing mindset to an all-or-something mindset? That perspective applies here too. So, don't let missing a day discourage you. The benefits are still all there waiting for you. Start up again, even with the smallest of steps.

Core points

- When an action becomes a habit, it doesn't take the same mental energy and willpower as it would as a one-off action.
- The most effective way to form habits is through the power of three: a cue, an action and a reward. The cue triggers the action and the reward reinforces it.
- Think about one habit you're trying to make automatic in your life – maybe it's daily movement – and a 'cue' you can set up as a useful reminder.

- When choosing your routine or action, follow the pillars of ACT – achievable, consistent and tailored – to set yourself up for success.
- Let's not forget your reward! Consider ways to track your progress and celebrate your successes. The pleasure centre of your brain will love it!

5

The right environment

Transform your space, transform your day

Having an environment that is supportive is really important for success.

Tory Burch

The modern workspace makes it easy to sit and sit and sit. Imagine your typical set-up – the desk adorned with neatly organised items, everything conveniently within arm's reach. Your computer sits prominently, the screen glowing with endless tasks and distractions. Your chair is comfortable and seemingly moulding to your body's shape, making it hard to resist.

The water bottle sitting on your desk ensures you never have to leave your seat for a drink. And why bother getting up for a phone call when your trusty device rests right next to your keyboard, always ready to connect you with the world? Oh, and let's not forget about the messaging apps that keep you glued to your screen, chatting away with colleagues without ever needing to rise from your seat. It's as if the workspace itself conspires to keep you firmly planted in a sedentary cocoon.

Wendy Wood is a distinguished social psychologist whose research has shed light on the fascinating field of habits and behaviour.

In *Good Habits, Bad Habits* Wood uncovers a crucial insight into human behaviour and habit formation using the example of smoking, which was widely accepted back in the day. Though many people were aware of its detrimental health effects, this knowledge alone wasn't enough to drastically reduce smoking rates. Despite the awareness of the risks, individuals struggled to quit this addictive habit.

The turning point came when society took action to change the environment surrounding smoking. Smoking bans were enforced in public places such as restaurants, bars and workplaces. Suddenly, smokers faced restrictions and the convenience of lighting up in various settings vanished. Smoking became harder – it required smokers to go outside and find designated areas to indulge in their habit. This transformation of the environment had a profound impact on smoking behaviour. The harmful habit was no longer as convenient and individuals found it more challenging to smoke without facing obstacles. As a result, smoking rates dramatically decreased, leading to a healthier, smoke-free environment.

Now let's apply this powerful concept to the modern challenge of prolonged sitting in the workplace. Similar to smoking, prolonged sitting is a habit many have developed over time. Although we know excessive sitting is detrimental to our health, breaking free from this sedentary routine can be tough.

The typical work environment is meticulously crafted for convenience, making it effortless to stay seated, immersing yourself in work while unintentionally neglecting your body's need for movement. However, just as policy makers changed the environment to discourage smoking, we can change our workspace to encourage movement.

As you design your active work hub, you're crafting an environment that opposes sedentary habits while also championing your overall wellbeing. This transformation reflects your commitment to infusing vitality and dynamism into your workday. Whether you incorporate one or several of the following concepts into your workspace, the magnitude of the change matters less than the intention behind it. Taking even a single step towards an active workspace holds immeasurable value, because progress in any form is a significant stride towards a healthier and more invigorated work life.

Your active work hub: how to design your desk space for optimum energy

By modifying your workspace and introducing elements that encourage movement, you can create an environment that supports your wellbeing and energises you throughout the day. You can strategically design your workspace to be an active work hub that prompts regular moments of movement and makes sitting for extended periods less convenient.

In this section I walk you through some simple principles that will help you transform your desk into an active work hub. These are all low- to no-cost adjustments designed to make your workspace energise you instead of lulling you into a stupor.

Items slightly out of reach

In your active work hub, everyday essentials are catalysts for movement. Place your pens, notepads and phone just out of reach. This simple tweak compels you to rise, stretch and actively retrieve these items when you need them, punctuating your workflow with bursts of physical engagement.

Active accessories

Elevate your workspace with tools that beckon you to move. This could involve adding lightweight dumbbells, resistance bands or even a stress ball that doubles as an exercise aid to your workspace. You can also transform ordinary items into movement enhancers; for example, two full water bottles or hefty reams of paper could become versatile weights. When taking a phone call or contemplating a task, seize the opportunity to engage in subtle movements using these active accessories, transforming those moments into micro-exercise sessions.

TRY THIS: water bottle workout

Get ready to turn your water bottle into your fitness buddy and bring some arm-strengthening into your workday routine. Whether you're on a conference call or chatting on the phone, this water bottle workout is the mini-movement solution for your busy day.

Let's dive into some **sideways arm circles** using a single water bottle – if you have two, you can do both arms at the same time. This is an easy way to give your arm muscles some love without breaking a sweat. Hold your water bottle in one hand. Extend that arm out to your side, parallel to the ground, and make small circles with your arm. These circles might look subtle, but they're working those shoulder and arm muscles. Do about ten to 20 circles, then switch directions for another round. Your arm will feel the gentle burn in no time. Change arms and repeat.

Now let's change it up with some **forward arm circles**. Hold your water bottle in one hand, but this time, extend your arm forward. Make those circles in front of you – like you're stirring a big cup of inspiration. Again, do ten to 20 circles in each direction, and then repeat with the other arm.

Movement break zones

Designate areas in your workspace for short movement breaks if space permits. Set up a corner for quick stretches, yoga poses or even a mini trampoline. These zones become retreats for energising breaks that refresh both body and mind.

Visual inspirations

Surround yourself with visual inspiration and cues that kindle your dedication to movement. Adorn your workspace with motivational quotes, a movement-inspired artwork or a photograph that communicates the significance of staying active. You could even create a vision board that inspires you to make self-care a priority. These visual additions serve as constant encouragement, reinforcing your commitment to movement.

You can even elevate your active work hub with cue cards that prompt you to get moving. Display your favourite chair stretches or exercises that can be done discreetly at your desk. Whether it's a poster illustrating rejuvenating stretches or a deck of cards suggesting various moves, these handy tools provide a visual reminder of the simple steps you can take to infuse movement into your workday. Check out the micro moves card deck at lizziewilliamson.com/active.

TRY THIS: visual reminders

Infuse the workspace with subtle movement cues. Place decals on staircases prompting stair use and employ floor markings guiding impromptu stretching routines. Consider using communal spaces such as the kitchen or photocopier area to display these prompts, gently nudging individuals towards movement throughout the day.

One office I know has my 'Energise while you boil!' poster in their kitchen to prompt people to get moving while they wait for the kettle to boil. It looks a little like this:

Energise while you boil!

Five energising micro moves:

1. **Stretch and breathe** – Reach for the stars! Stretch your arms up high and take a deep breath. Exhale stress away as you wait.
2. **Power push-ups** – Turn up the heat on your muscles! Drop and give us ten push-ups against the countertop. You'll feel the burn before the kettle does!
3. **Active breathing** – Inhale calmness, exhale stress. Close your eyes, take deep breaths and let your worries steam away. You've got this!
4. **Calf raises dance** – Boil and bounce! Lift those heels and dance on your toes. Get your legs moving and blood pumping for a kettle-full of energy.

5. **Gratitude pause** – Brew up some positivity! Take a moment to be grateful for the small things. A thankful heart makes every cup sweeter.

Turn kettle time into 'me' time with these quick and fun breaks. Your body and mind will thank you.

Stay energised, stay awesome!

Download your free copy of this poster and others at lizziewilliamson.com/active.

Taking your active work hub to the next level

Depending on your resources – time, space and funds – you may be able to take your active work hub to the next level with equipment specifically designed to boost your workday movement. Here are some suggestions for equipment that require additional investment. There are pros and cons to each of these suggestions, so do your research to figure out which might be right for you. In case the additional investment required to introduce the pieces of equipment isn't on the cards for you or your company right now, I've also included budget busters for each suggestion – ideas for how to improvise to achieve a similar outcome without heading to the shops.

The rise of stand-up desks: from peculiar to practical

We've all heard about the benefits of stand-up desks, but let's get one thing straight: standing all day isn't the holy grail. It's about finding the sweet spot that balances sitting, standing and moving. Here's the secret sauce – a stand-up desk is not about just standing still. With a stand-up desk, or a stand-up desk converter, you're free to move, shift and groove. You can sway side to side, do a little happy dance or simply shift your weight from one leg to the other.

Standing in the same position for hours on end can have its own challenges – hello, sore feet and achy legs. That's why the beauty of the stand-up desk is in the alternation it facilitates. It's like a dance, switching between sitting, standing and moving, giving your body the variation it craves. When you stand, you engage your muscles, improve your posture and boost your circulation. Then, when you sit, you give those standing muscles a break and let your body rest. The other benefit of spending some time standing is that your body naturally tends to move more.

Budget buster: I piled books and boxes on my regular desk to turn it into a stand-up desk for years – it works a treat.

TRY THIS: stand-up desk micro moves

Standing doesn't mean you have to stay static. In fact, the standing position can provide a fantastic opportunity to introduce a burst of subtle physical activity into your workday. Remember to perform these exercises within your comfort zone and consider your workspace set-up. These quick moves can help you stay active and invigorated while working at your stand-up desk:

- **Basic heel raises** are a great way to get moving at your stand-up desk and boost circulation. Stand upright near your desk and lift your heels, balancing on the balls of your feet. Hold this for a few seconds, then lower your heels back down. Repeat this ten to 15 times.
- **Sideways leg raises** activate your hip abductors, improve balance and reduce tension in your lower body. Start by standing near your desk and extending your right leg out to the side with your big toe on the floor. Engage your core and lift your straight leg up to whatever height feels comfortable, and then lower it back down. Repeat this ten to 20 times and then change legs.
- **Forward leg raises** are excellent for activating lower body muscles and maintaining circulation. Start by extending your right leg forward with your toes resting on the floor. Engage your core muscles to help with stability and lift your right leg upward to a comfortable height. Lower your leg back down and repeat the move ten to 20 times before switching to the other leg.

Stride into the future: embracing treadmill desks

Now let's kick it up a notch and introduce a tool that might not yet be as mainstream as stand-up desks but has the potential to revolutionise your work routine: treadmill desks or walking pads for under your stand-up desk. You're not just standing; you're also walking – right at your desk! Treadmill desks or walking pads provide a symphony of productivity and fitness. They're redefining how we perceive work, combining the benefits of movement and focus into one beneficial experience.

Treadmill desks or walking pads let you walk at a comfortable pace while you type emails, brainstorm ideas or ace that presentation. They take your workday to a whole new level, where movement fuels your creativity and keeps your energy levels going strong.

I know what you might be thinking: *Walking while working? Won't that be distracting?* Surprisingly, it's quite the opposite. As you'll hear all about in the second part of this book (which concerns your active workday toolkit), walking boosts your focus and creativity. It can also help reduce stress and anxiety, providing a natural rhythm that can help you stay calm and composed even during the busiest of workdays. It's like turning your desk into a stress-busting sanctuary.

Budget buster: stand up and walk on the spot or pace the room any chance you get.

Seated fitness: the under-desk elliptical

If standing up or walking while working isn't quite feasible for you, there's a piece of equipment on the market that keeps you walking while performing your tasks: the under-desk elliptical. This portable piece of exercise equipment lets you keep your legs moving in a gentle elliptical motion while seated. The magic lies in the fact that your upper body can stay focused on your desk tasks while your legs get their dose of activity. It's multitasking for your wellbeing.

Budget buster: place some books under your desk and alternate taping your left and right toes on the books.

Footrests: unassuming and underrated

The addition of a footrest to your workspace can bring a range of benefits you might not have even considered. Footrests – unassuming and underrated pieces of equipment – encourage you to adopt a more natural sitting position, allowing your feet to rest flat and your hips to align properly. The angle and elevation they provide can help alleviate pressure on your lower back, promoting better spinal alignment and reducing discomfort.

You can also use a footrest to your active advantage. For example, you can walk your feet up and down as you're sitting, or alternate tapping your left and right toes on top of it. These subtle movements can help keep your leg muscles engaged and your blood circulating, preventing the lethargy that often accompanies prolonged sitting.

Budget buster: make your own footrest using a small and sturdy box, a stack of books or a couple of firm cushions.

Ergonomic chairs: elevating your sitting experience

An ergonomic chair typically offers adjustable seat height, backrest angle, lumbar support, armrest height and even seat depth. Personalising these elements allows you to ensure that your spine maintains its natural curvature, your arms rest comfortably and your posture remains aligned throughout your workday – together with some movement, of course! An additional back rest can also be used. It's important to note that every body is unique and what works for one person may not work for another. Finding the right chair is about discovering what keeps your body safe, comfortable and happy.

Budget buster: experiment with adding a cushion to the seat of your chair or behind your lower back to allow a more natural seated position.

Rethinking seating: balance balls and kneeling chairs

Imagine occasionally swapping out your regular office chair for something a bit unconventional yet incredibly effective. My first suggestion is to sit on a fitball (also known as a Swiss ball or gym ball) for short periods of time. This innovative seating option challenges the status quo by introducing an element of playfulness to your work set-up. Instead of a traditional chair, you'll find yourself perched atop a blown-up ball that's designed to engage your core muscles while you work. The magic of the fitball chair lies in its dynamic nature. As you sit on the ball, your body instinctively makes micro-adjustments to maintain stability. These subtle movements activate your core muscles, promoting better posture and preventing the onset of that all-too-familiar midday slouch.

Another intriguing active seating option is the kneeling chair. This chair defies conventional sitting by encouraging a more open and upright posture. Instead of the traditional seat and backrest, a kneeling chair features angled supports for your shins and knees, allowing your hips to be positioned at a forward tilt. The beauty of the kneeling chair lies in its ability to naturally align your spine and pelvis, and also in its claims to reduce the strain on your lower back. While kneeling chairs might not be suitable for everyone, they offer a unique and valuable addition to an ergonomic workspace, promoting better posture and minimising discomfort.

While spending your entire workday on these alternative chairs might not be the goal, consider the benefits of swapping them in from time to time. Mixing up how you sit allows your body to experience different postures and engage various muscle groups, breaking up the monotony of prolonged sitting. Remember, as we're all different, this is about figuring out what works for your body. Speak to an allied health professional for recommendations tailored to your specific body and circumstances.

Core points

- The modern workspace is designed for you to sit, sit and sit, putting perceived productivity and output above wellness. It's time to change that!

- What habits does your workspace make easy and difficult? Is everything you need in easy reach, meaning you never have to rise from your chair?
- Small steps – such as moving files to the other side of the room so you have to stand to retrieve them – can add up to create a more flexible and agile body.
- If you want to take it to the next level, explore the world of stand-up desks and active accessories.
- If space allows, designate areas of your workspace for short movement breaks. For example, you might have a yoga mat rolled out next to your desk, ready and waiting for you.

Part II
Redesign
The active workday toolkit

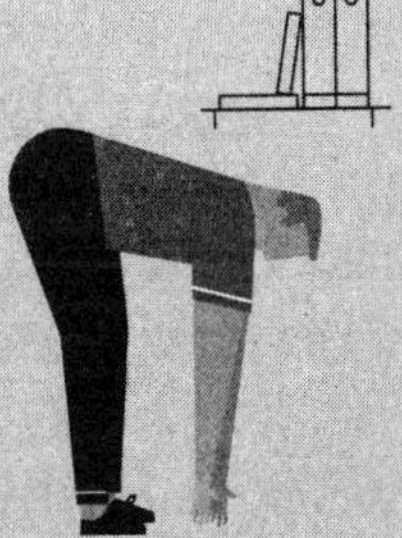

The active workday toolkit is a unique approach to transforming your day through quick moments of movement and mindfulness, or what I like to call 'micro moves'.

Think of this part of *The Active Workday Advantage* as a set of tools for tackling the challenges of your workday. It explains when and how to seamlessly incorporate micro moves into your daily routine for maximum impact. These quick and easy moments serve as specialised tools, meticulously crafted to break the monotony of a sedentary workday and cater to your body, mind, energy levels and overall mindset. They empower you to navigate the demands of your day with resilience and vitality. Just as a skilled craftsman chooses the right tool for the job, you can pick from your array of micro moves to address specific needs. For example:

- Need a mental pick-me up? Try a micro-breather break (see chapter 6).
- Facing a challenging problem? Take a 30-second walk on the spot (see chapter 6).
- Feeling sluggish and low on energy? Try a posture check-up (see chapter 7).
- Getting distracted by tightness in your neck and shoulders? Engage in some sneaky chair stretches (see chapter 8).

Empowering your workday with micro moves

As you continue reading, you'll discover how to harness the power of micro moves at key moments in your workday. Each chapter in this part of the book will provide insights, strategies and practical tips for optimising your performance and wellbeing through movement – and it doesn't have to be complicated.

This is a straightforward guide that explains when and how to effectively integrate micro moves into your routine. Whether it's a 30-second stretch, a quick walk around the office or a posture boost, these small actions can have a significant impact on your overall health and performance. Open your toolkit, choose your micro move and get ready to experience the active workday advantage.

Let's take a look at what's inside:

- **Activate your brain.** When a mental boost is in order, choose a brain-boosting micro move from your toolkit. Just as a well-timed strategy ups your game, these brain boosts uplift your mind. Think of it as mental dynamism – these micro moves ignite neural pathways, increasing your cognitive agility, problem-solving skills and innovative thinking.
- **Change your mind.** Research shows that the way you hold and move your body can make a substantial difference to how you feel. Just as posture and physical strength are crucial for your overall wellbeing, they also play a significant role in shaping your mindset.
- **Take care of your body.** Engage in body-boosting micro moves that stretch and rejuvenate your muscles, enhance your posture and reduce the risk of discomfort. These actions serve as a daily investment in your body's health, ensuring you feel your best and can perform at your peak throughout the workday.
- **Improve your mood.** For an instant mood lift, turn to your toolkit. When challenges arise and your spirits need elevation, a mood-boosting micro move is your solution. Movement triggers the release of endorphins, infusing positivity and a sense of accomplishment. Feel your mood brighten with each moment.
- **Vitalise your energy.** As the day progresses and energy dwindles, your toolkit offers a boost. Instead of relying on external stimulants, opt for a micro move to reactivate your energy. These bursts of motion enhance circulation, oxygenate your brain and rejuvenate your body, all without the sugar crash.

- **Elevate connections.** It's not just about strengthening bonds at work but also about bringing some fun and joy into the workday. Engage in shared activities with colleagues, enhancing teamwork and fostering a positive work atmosphere with connection-boosting micro moves.

Get set for a workday that's truly active – in every sense!

Where to begin

Start by incorporating one aspect of the toolkit before, during or after work situations that you want to see improvement in. Perhaps your first step could be trying out some energising movement that gets your blood flowing before an important meeting, or maybe some mindful breathing that helps you find calm amid the chaos after a stressful presentation. Experiment with different tools and observe how they impact your wellbeing and productivity in those moments.

Remember, you're not expected to tackle everything at once. Just as a pit-stop crew focuses on the immediate needs of a car during a race, you can prioritise the techniques that address your current challenges and goals. Take it one step at a time, gradually expanding your practice as you experience the positive effects.

Together, we'll create a harmonious and balanced approach that puts you at an advantage when you need it most. Whether you need to energise yourself to complete a challenging task or reset after a high-stress situation, this active workday toolkit is your companion for success. One micro move at a time, we'll drive you towards a more productive, fulfilling and active workday.

6

Activate your brain

A reboot for peak performance

If you take care of your mind, you take care of the world.

Arianna Huffington

In the modern workplace, the demand for mental sharpness and cognitive agility is relentless. Whether you're tackling complex projects, participating in brainstorming sessions or solving intricate problems, your brain is your most valuable asset. However, maintaining a consistently high level of cognitive performance throughout the workday can be challenging.

Mental energy is a finite resource. As you engage in tasks demanding sustained attention, problem-solving and decision-making, your mental energy gradually depletes. The outcome is mental fatigue – a noticeable reduction in cognitive performance due to decreased focus, heightened distractibility and difficulty maintaining attention, which can have a significant impact on your overall productivity and the quality of your work.

Life has become inextricably intertwined with digital technologies. This constant connectivity exposes us to an unending stream of information, including emails, social media updates and news alerts. Coping with this ceaseless information flow can be overwhelming for the brain, often leading to cognitive strain.

Furthermore, many of us attempt to multitask, simultaneously juggling multiple tasks and sources of information, which can further overwhelm the brain and hinder cognitive performance.

As we've already discussed, many of today's jobs require us to sit at a desk for prolonged periods. Unfortunately, this can lead to physical stagnation, which in turn reduces blood flow to the brain. Diminished blood flow can result in impaired cognitive function and contribute to mental fatigue. This sedentary behaviour exacerbates issues caused by poor posture and uncomfortable workspaces, leading to physical discomfort that can distract us and divert cognitive resources away from important tasks.

Stress and pressure are inherent in the modern workplace and are often triggered by the demands of deadlines, high expectations and intense workloads. In response to stress, the body releases cortisol, a hormone that can impair cognitive function when elevated for extended periods. High stress levels can also lead to anxiety, difficulties in making decisions and problems with memory. High-pressure situations, such as important presentations or negotiations, can create anxiety, which can disrupt cognitive performance, hindering clear thinking precisely when it's needed the most.

The absence of adequate mental breaks during the workday can lead to mental exhaustion. As mental fatigue sets in, the brain's capacity for problem-solving, creativity and efficient decision-making diminishes significantly. Moreover, a persistent lack of mental breaks can contribute to burnout, characterised by emotional and physical exhaustion. Burnout poses a severe threat to cognitive performance, overall wellbeing and the ability to engage effectively in work.

This is where the concept of activating your brain comes into play. Activating your brain means infusing it with the energy and focus required to excel in your tasks. It's about staying mentally sharp, alert and creative, even when faced with demanding situations. One effective way to achieve this is through the strategic use of brain-boosting micro moves.

Harnessing the power of brain-boosting micro moves

Picture this. You've been working diligently on your computer for hours. Your eyes are fixed on the screen and your fingers are typing away. Despite your best efforts, you start to feel your attention slipping and your mind struggling to stay focused. Mental fog sets in, hindering your productivity. Fear not, because there's a powerful solution: a well-timed brain boost.

A brain-boosting micro move can be as simple as closing your eyes and taking a few deep breaths, or engaging in a quick physical activity such as stretching or going for a short walk. These activities allow us to disengage from the immediate demands of work while still priming our minds for optimal performance. Brain boosts are small, intentional actions that can have a profound impact on your cognitive functioning. Stretching and walking, for example, enhance blood circulation. Increased blood flow means more oxygen and nutrients reach your brain, helping it to function optimally. Brain boosts also help to alleviate stress – a common cognitive roadblock – reducing cortisol levels and promoting a state of calm focus conducive to creative and analytical thinking.

Certain micro moves, such as walking, can stimulate creative thinking. They encourage your brain to break free from rigid thought patterns and explore new avenues of imagination. As Jae, a seasoned creative director, shared with me:

> *Before diving into a brainstorming session, I make it a ritual to do a short freestyle dance. It sounds unconventional, but it loosens up my mind and allows ideas to flow freely. The difference it makes in my brainstorming sessions is astounding.*

You'll also discover they can act as mental resets to enhance focus. When you're stuck on a problem or feeling mentally fatigued, taking a moment for a micro move can reinvigorate your brain and improve concentration.

When to make a brain-boosting micro move

You may have heard that 'brain breaks' are being used in schools – and with good reason. I'm always telling my teenagers that if they want to be at an advantage for an exam they should do some physical activity – or, as I like to call it, a 'brain boost' – beforehand, especially if the exam is in the afternoon! One study revealed that cognitive fatigue tends to set in towards the end of the day, resulting in a notable decline in test performance. In fact, for every passing hour, test scores decreased by the equivalent of ten days of learning. But there's good news: incorporating brain breaks into the routine not only eliminated this decline but actually improved performance.

Now, you may not be doing exams in your workplace, but the implications of this research extend beyond the classroom. Just like students at school, adults in the workplace experience cognitive fatigue, which can affect their productivity and focus throughout the day. Incorporating brain boosts into your work routine can help combat this decline and enhance your ability to produce high-quality work. According to a review published in 2022, brief breaks have a significant impact on reducing mental fatigue and boosting vigour, which refers to the willingness to persevere when faced with challenging work.

Just imagine the advantage this can give you in your work. As the day progresses, you have the power to counteract cognitive fatigue by making strategic, brain-boosting micro moves that serve as mental recharges, allowing you to maintain your productivity and perform at your best.

Here are five other key moments when brain boosts can help your brain to operate at its peak:

1. **Starting a new project** often requires intense concentration and the ability to rapidly process information. Take a brain boost to ensure your mind is sharp and ready to tackle the task at hand effectively.

2. Creativity and idea generation require cognitive flexibility. Activate your brain with a brain boost **before a brainstorming session** to enhance your ability to think more freely and generate innovative ideas.
3. **Tackling complex problems and challenging tasks** demands sustained focus and problem-solving abilities. Prepare your brain with a brain boost to be engaged and firing on all cylinders.
4. **Handling a high-stakes decision or negotiation** requires a sharp mind and the ability to make sound judgements. Use a brain boost to boost your energy, motivation and cognitive clarity, ensuring you approach high-stakes situations with confidence.
5. Before **carrying out tedious data entry or repetitive tasks**, take a brain boost to combat the physical strain of prolonged sitting and refresh your mind. This makes the task more manageable, reduces physical discomfort and mental fatigue, and helps you to maintain focus and accuracy.

Don't underestimate the power of these small moments. Incorporating brain boosts into your daily routine can make a world of difference to your productivity, creativity and overall wellbeing. So, the next time you feel your brain reaching its limits or you want to set the stage for success, remember the incredible benefits of these rejuvenating pauses. Give yourself permission to take a step back for a few minutes or seconds, recharge and return to your work with a fresh perspective.

Brain boost 1: creativity charger

In the pursuit of productivity, we often find ourselves trying to stay switched on constantly and pushing ourselves to the limit. Our brains have a remarkable capacity for generating ideas and solving problems; however, prolonged periods of intense focus on a single task can lead to mental fatigue and a decline in cognitive performance.

Our thinking narrows and we struggle to see alternative perspectives or think creatively.

Getting active can help us overcome this challenge. Research suggests that incorporating physical activity into our work routine can actually significantly increase creative thinking and problem-solving skills, leading to improved performance of tasks that require innovative thinking. As Henry David Thoreau, one of the US's most foremost nature writers, wrote, 'Methinks that the moment my legs begin to move, my thoughts begin to flow'.

So, why exactly does getting moving have such a positive impact on our creativity? Well, let's dive into the science behind it. Engaging in physical activity is like giving your brain a turbocharge. Your heart pumps faster, sending blood filled with oxygen and essential nutrients to your brain. This boost in circulation doesn't just help you feel more alert; it's like a mental workout, promoting neuroplasticity, which means your brain can create new connections and get smarter. It's like fertiliser for your brain cells, nurturing their growth and maintenance.

Physical activity also allows our brains to tap into what is called the 'default mode network'. This is responsible for creative thinking, daydreaming and making connections between seemingly unrelated ideas. When we get moving, we activate the default mode network, enabling us to make new connections, think more divergently and explore innovative solutions.

Additionally, movement helps to alleviate stress and mental fatigue, which can be significant barriers to creativity. When we're stressed, our cognitive resources are depleted and we struggle to think clearly and creatively. By taking moments to move, we give ourselves a chance to reduce stress levels, allowing our creative juices to flow more freely.

The next time you're craving a creative boost, ditch your computer for a moment and embark on an activity to help your brain thrive – move, take a walk and let the magic happen!

TRY THIS: ignite creativity with a micro walk

Ever wondered why, when you're stuck on an idea or a decision and you go for a walk, you get that moment of clarity? Research from Stanford University has revealed that walking can have a profound impact on boosting creativity, regardless of whether or not you're outside. In the study, participants who engaged in walking experienced an impressive 60 per cent increase in their creative output compared to those who remained seated, and those creative juices continued to flow for hours after sitting back down. As Shane O'Mara writes in *In Praise of Walking: The new science of how we walk and why it's good for us*, when we move around, 'activity spreads across more distant brain regions – increasing the likelihood that half-thoughts and quarter-ideas, sitting below consciousness, can come together in new combinations'.

When you find yourself stuck in a creative rut, break free with a walk, even if you're confined to your workspace. Consider incorporating walking into your work-related interactions. Instead of catching up for a sit-down meeting, suggest a 'walk and talk' session. When appropriate, opt for walking or pacing while on the phone instead of sitting down. These simple adjustments not only keep you physically active but can also lead to more dynamic and productive conversations.

If circumstances prevent you from stepping outside, don't worry. You can still reap the rewards with a walk on the spot by following these instructions:

1. Using the stopwatch on your phone to keep time, walk on the spot for 30 seconds.
2. Now imagine it's a sunny day at the beach and you're walking on hot sand. Walk on the spot for 30 seconds, trying to keep your feet on the ground for as little time as possible.
3. Go back to a regular-pace walk on the spot for 30 seconds.
4. Repeat the hot sand walk (or jog) for another 30 seconds.

By incorporating micro walks into your routine, you can access your innate creativity and find new ways to approach challenges. Let your imagination soar as you ignite your creativity step by step.

Brain boost 2: focus finder

In the hustle and bustle of our daily lives, it can feel counterproductive to add more obligations to our already jam-packed workdays. However, an intriguing study suggests that taking short mental breaks can be the key to unlocking your true focus potential. Rather than hindering productivity, these breaks dramatically improve your ability to concentrate on tasks for extended periods.

This research presents a challenge to a world that glorifies non-stop work and endless productivity. It suggests that grinding through tasks without pause might not be the way to go. Rather, taking short, intentional breaks can actually boost your overall productivity and enhance your ability to concentrate. These breaks allow your brain to reset, recharge and refocus, making it easier to tackle even the most demanding of tasks with renewed focus and clarity. So, take a moment to stand up, walk briskly and tap your way to a renewed sense of focus and productivity.

TRY THIS: the tap-20 refocus

When you find yourself getting distracted during your busy day, the tap-20 refocus exercise is the perfect solution. This brain-boosting micro move combines brisk walking with tactile engagement, allowing you to break away from your seated position and refresh your mind and body. By standing up and moving around your workspace with energy and purpose, you'll invigorate your senses and combat the effects of digital overload. Let's get started.

Take a break from your seated position and stand up. Begin by briskly walking around your workspace – whether it's your office or your home – while maintaining an energetic pace. Choose 20 objects within your reach and tap them lightly as you walk. Look around and identify various objects in your immediate surroundings that you can tap. These could include your desk, your chair, a door handle, a wall or a decorative item. The goal is to tap each object quickly and move on to the next one.

Aim to tap objects at different heights to make the exercise more engaging and dynamic. Reach up and tap objects that are above your shoulder level, such as shelves, cabinets or the top of a doorframe. Bend down or squat slightly to tap objects at or below your waist level, such as chair legs or the base of a desk. And don't forget to tap objects at a comfortable middle height, such as tabletops, countertops or the middle of a wall.

The tap-20 brain-boosting move is a brief yet impactful way to reset your focus and re-energise yourself. It allows you to step away from the digital world, engage with your physical environment and tap into a more switched-on brain.

Brain boost 3: performance enhancer

Imagine your mind as a sophisticated computer tirelessly processing an infinite stream of data throughout your workday. Just like any computer, it can experience moments of overload, causing the system to slow down, freeze or even crash.

As the demands of your job pile up, your mental state can begin to resemble a complex machine running hot. The more tasks you take on, the higher the stress levels rise. With overload comes stress, and stress has a way of infiltrating every aspect of your work life. It's like a fog that clouds your judgement, slows your reaction time and impedes your ability to think clearly. It compromises the very qualities that you rely on to excel at work, including focus, creativity and decision-making.

Just as a computer requires an occasional reset to function optimally, your mind needs a moment of stillness and recalibration to find clarity amid the chaos. The good news is that there is a powerful tool you can use to navigate the complex circuitry of your mind: the micro breather. This involves using your own breath to get yourself back on track.

Take a breather: your mind's reboot button

You might have heard of 'micro breaks', but I prefer to call them 'micro breathers' for a specific reason: the term 'break' implies the need for an extended pause, which can be a turn-off for the many of us who feel we don't have the luxury to take breaks during our workday. The pressure of work, lack of permission and time restraints can make us resistant to the idea of stopping.

By adopting the term 'micro *breather*' I aim to emphasise that these activities are quick, efficient and purposeful. They're designed to enhance your cognitive functioning without demanding significant time or disrupting your workflow. In essence, they're about maximising productivity and wellbeing within the confines of your busy schedule. So, while you may be reluctant to take traditional *breaks*, incorporating these *breathers* can help you stay sharp, focused and energised throughout your workday.

Back to the science now, there are mountains of evidence supporting the benefits of taking micro breathers throughout the workday. For example, a study conducted by Microsoft's Human Factors Lab focusing on the effects of virtual fatigue revealed that incorporating short breaks between back-to-back meetings can prevent the accumulation of stress and provide employees with an opportunity to reset and refresh. Another study looking at how breaks can impact the job performance of call centre workers found that short cognitive breaks led to improved sales.

It's important to recognise, though, that not all breaks are created equal. Mindlessly scrolling through social media or getting lost in random videos may provide temporary distraction, but they don't necessarily reactivate our brain. Instead of sinking time and energy into something that isn't going to help us work – or feel – any better, micro breathers are about engaging in activities that revitalise our minds and redirect our focus to the task at hand.

When you notice your mental operating system getting sluggish, thoughts running wild and decision-making coming to a halt, it's time to hit your mind's reboot button. Micro breathers act as a cognitive reset, fostering a state of mindfulness that activates the brain's executive functions. Stress hormones decrease, the mind stills and cognitive performance is enhanced. The reset activates the prefrontal cortex, which is responsible for decision-making, problem-solving and focus, allowing you to make informed choices with greater clarity.

By taking regular moments to reset your brain, you can preserve your cognitive abilities, sustain your focus and ensure consistent, high-quality output throughout the day. You'll be on your way to achieving an A in productivity.

TRY THIS: take a micro breather

In the fast-paced world of work, stress can build to the point that you begin to feel like a pressure cooker about to burst. These micro-breathers serve as a release valve, resetting your mental state, reducing stress and helping you regain clarity. Practising and employing these strategies will help you to manage various work scenarios, balance your emotions and optimise your cognitive performance.

Strategy 1: box breathing

Use box breathing when you're facing a critical decision-making moment or need to regain composure in high-pressure situations at work.

Box breathing involves inhaling, holding the breath, exhaling and again holding the breath, each for a count of four. Each cycle can be visualised as a square – the inhale represented by an up-stroke, the first hold by a perpendicular line, the exhale by a down-stroke and the second hold by a line returning you to your starting position. The deliberate rhythm calms the nervous system, reduces the production of stress hormones and allows you to regain control of your thoughts, increasing your focus, clarity and ability to make informed decisions under pressure.

Visualising the square, follow these instructions to give box breathing a try:

1. Inhale deeply through your nose for a count of four.
2. Hold your breath for a count of four.
3. Exhale slowly and completely through your mouth for a count of four.
4. Hold your breath for another count of four.
5. Repeat this cycle for several rounds, focusing your attention on the breath and the counting.

Strategy 2: deep belly breathing

Use deep belly breathing when you're dealing with stress or tension that's affecting your emotional state and making it hard to approach challenging conversations and situations with a clear mind.

When stress and tension are high – for example, when you're about to have a difficult conversation with a colleague – your body responds by triggering the fight-or-flight response, which can hinder effective communication. Deep belly breathing counteracts this response by calming the nervous system, allowing you to approach situations with a sense of calm and openness, leading to better communication and conflict resolution.

These are the steps for using deep belly breathing to reduce stress and promote relaxation:

1. Sit or stand comfortably with your feet shoulder-width apart.
2. Place your hands gently on your abdomen.
3. Close your eyes or soften your gaze.
4. Inhale deeply and slowly through your nose, allowing your abdomen to rise like a gentle wave.
5. Exhale slowly and completely through your mouth, feeling your abdomen sink back down.
6. Focus on the sensation of your breath and the movement of your diaphragm.
7. Continue this deep belly breathing for several breath cycles, letting go of tension with each exhalation.

Strategy 3: counted breaths

Use the counted breaths technique when your mind is racing with distractions and you need to regain focus and concentration.

Counted breaths is a mindfulness practice that brings your attention to the present moment. By counting your breaths, you redirect your focus and quieten mental chatter. This allows you to then refocus on your tasks, increasing productivity and mental clarity.

Follow these instructions to regain focus and concentration:

1. Begin to take slow, deep breaths.
2. As you inhale, silently count 'one' in your mind.
3. As you exhale, count 'two'.
4. Continue counting each inhale and exhale, up to a count of ten. Remember it's not the length of the breath you are counting but the number of breaths.
5. If your mind begins to wander or thoughts intrude, gently bring your focus back to the breathing and counting.
6. Once you reach ten, start again at one if you wish to continue.

Core points

- The absence of adequate mental breaks during the workday can lead to mental exhaustion, affecting our ability to problem-solve, harness creativity and make confident decisions.
- An active workday is the antidote, reinvigorating not only your body but also your mental performance.
- Integrate brain-boosting micro moves into your day by doing something as simple as closing your eyes and taking a few deep breaths or going for a short walk. Afterwards, notice if your head feels clearer or creativity comes more easily.
- Instead of seeing movement as something that takes you away from your work, recognise that taking a 'breather' can actually increase your output.

7

Change your mind

Embracing the power of mindset

If you don't like something, change it. If you can't change it, change your attitude.

Maya Angelou

In the unpredictable world of work, we've all encountered challenging moments that put our composure and confidence to the test. From project setbacks to customer difficulties and organisational changes, how we respond to these situations can significantly impact our professional success. Our state of mind – the emotional and mental space we inhabit – can be the ultimate determinant of our performance, productivity and overall experience in the workplace, influencing how we interpret and react to events and situations. Our state of mind is the lens through which we perceive challenges and opportunities, setbacks and achievements. It shapes our attitude, behaviour and decision-making.

Consider two colleagues preparing to speak at a crucial meeting, each tasked with presenting a bold, innovative idea. One colleague approaches the podium with trembling hands and a racing heart, her mind clouded by nerves and self-doubt. The other colleague strides forward with confidence and a calm demeanour, radiating assurance in her idea's potential. The first colleague's state of mind is marked by nervousness, self-criticism and a fear of judgement. She stumbles over her words, her message lost in a haze of anxiety. In contrast, the second colleague's state of mind is marked by self-assuredness, clarity and resilience. She navigates the presentation with ease, her idea shining through her poised delivery.

A positive state of mind is not about being blindly optimistic or suppressing negative emotions. It's about cultivating emotional intelligence and resilience. It's the ability to acknowledge negative emotions, understand their root causes and channel them constructively. It's the capacity to adapt to the ups and downs of work with grace. A workplace filled with individuals who can harness the power of their emotional states is likely to foster creativity, collaboration and innovation. Such individuals can manage stress effectively, inspire confidence in their colleagues and bounce back from setbacks stronger than before.

What if you could actively control your mindset and turn negative feelings into positive feelings? Imagine having tools to guide you through your workday's emotional challenges. That's where mindset moves come in. They help you to leverage your emotions for better outcomes. Your state of mind isn't just along for the ride; it drives your professional path. By mastering these small mindset-boosting micro moves, you take control of your emotional journey at work, which leads to greater success and satisfaction.

With three mindset-focused micro moves and a whole toolbox of gratitude practices for you to try in this chapter, you'll gain the tools to transform your state of mind when facing the challenges of your workday. You'll be able to convert nervousness into confidence, self-doubt into self-assuredness and a lack of motivation into a strong sense of purpose. Let's dive in.

Mindset move 1: kickstart your workday

The demands of life, both at home and at work, can leave us feeling disconnected and disengaged as we start our workday. Overwhelm, family responsibilities, financial stressors and the constant juggling act of work-life balance can weigh heavily on our minds, making it difficult to muster focus and motivation.

A morning mindset reset is a powerful solution. Before you dive into your emails or your to-do list, take a moment for yourself to kickstart your workday. This practice ensures that you begin your workday on the right foot – full of enthusiasm and with a clear sense of purpose. By incorporating it into your morning routine, you're making a conscious effort to shift from a state of disconnection and uncertainty to a state of increased engagement and focus, even when facing external pressures.

This simple yet effective morning ritual can act as a catalyst for a more productive and satisfying workday. It helps you centre yourself and set positive intentions, and invigorates both your body and your mind, readying you to tackle the day ahead.

TRY THIS: the mindset reset

This mindset reset is about cultivating a positive mindset and energising yourself for the challenges ahead. I had the incredible opportunity to be part of a conference at which the Dalai Lama, renowned for his wisdom, shared his belief that 'an open heart is an open mind'. By taking a few moments to centre yourself, choose a positive focus and open yourself up to the day ahead, you're not only preparing yourself for a productive workday but also embracing a holistic approach to your work that extends beyond completing tasks and meeting deadlines. It's about recognising that work is an opportunity for personal growth and contributing to a greater purpose.

As you settle into your workspace, it's easy to get swept up in the rush of daily obligations. However, what if you took a moment to set yourself up with a positive, energised mindset? Don't worry; we won't delve into the mystical and esoteric here. Instead, let's try a quick and practical mindset reset to get you into the groove. Are you ready?

1. **Breathe and let go.** Begin by taking a deep breath in. Then, as you exhale slowly, release any tension or stress that may have

accumulated during the morning rush. Close your eyes or soften your gaze and feel an immediate sense of relief and relaxation.

2. **Move inward.** Slowly drop your chin towards your chest, allowing your shoulders to follow suit as your body rolls forward naturally. In this folded-forward position, imagine the weight you've been carrying on your shoulders trickling away.
3. **Say 'yes' – and 'no'.** Give your head a gentle shake from side to side, as if saying 'no', and picture one thing you want to decline today, such as taking on additional work you don't have time for. Then, counter that by gently nodding your head, visualising one thing you want to say 'yes' to today, such as accepting a new project that aligns with your goals or interests.
4. **Find your centre.** Engage your abdominal muscles as you gradually roll back up, taking your time to bring your head back upright to avoid dizziness. Visualise a point within your body – perhaps around your heart or abdomen – radiating with warm, glowing light. Let this light fill you with a sense of inner harmony. No need for mystical chants; just establish a simple connection with your core.
5. **Choose your mindset mantra.** Take a moment to consider the tasks, projects or interactions you'll face today. Acknowledge any potential challenges or obstacles. Create a short, empowering statement that resonates with you; for example, *I embrace challenges*, *I'm a productivity powerhouse* or *I am capable of achieving great things*. Repeat this mantra silently, directing its positive energy towards the radiant light you visualised at your core. Allow it to fuel your motivation and self-belief, even if you have to 'fake it till you make it'!

Mindset move 2: confident body language

Have you ever found yourself in a critical work situation in which you needed to make an important phone call or voice your opinion, only to be held back by self-doubt and uncertainty? The nagging inner critic creeps in, whispering that you're not good enough, and your confidence takes a nosedive. In those challenging moments, a simple yet remarkably effective trick can come to your rescue.

Your body and mind are deeply connected, and the way you hold yourself physically can impact your mental state significantly. Numerous studies have highlighted the profound impact of posture and body language on our mood and how others perceive us. At the time of writing, 'Your body language may shape who you are' by social psychologist Amy Cuddy is the second most viewed TED Talk ever. It underscores the transformative power of the physical. When we stand tall with our shoulders back and our heads held high, we send a potent message to both brain and body that we are confident and capable. Plus, when others see us exuding confidence through our body language, they are more inclined to perceive us as solid and competent.

In the modern workplace, many of us spend the majority of our days in a contracted position. We're hunched over our desks, staring at phones and computers, our bodies constricted in a way that hardly reflects confidence and power. Our physical posture informs our mental state – small and vulnerable. But it doesn't have to be this way.

Imagine yourself before a high-stakes meeting. Your heart may be racing and self-doubt might be creeping in. Instead of slouching or hunching over, straighten your spine, square your shoulders and take up space in the room. As you consciously adjust your body posture, you're not just sending signals to those around you that you're ready and capable; you're also reprogramming your own mindset. You're telling yourself that you have the authority and confidence to handle the task at hand.

The next time you need to make an important phone call, contribute to a crucial discussion, ace a job interview, impress in a client meeting, deliver a compelling speech or seal the deal in a sales pitch, try the following mindset-boosting micro move to project confidence and make a more impactful impression. You've got this!

TRY THIS: the posture power-up

In the dynamic world of business, where confidence and authority are paramount, mastering your posture is the key to unlocking your professional potential. Introducing the posture power-up – a game-changing technique that empowers you to unleash your professional presence, fast. Whether you do it at your desk before logging on to a virtual meeting or find a quiet corner (many people choose the bathroom), by incorporating this simple yet transformative practice into your daily routine you'll project an air of competence, establish credibility and command attention like never before. Prepare to power-up your posture with these easy steps:

1. **Take a mindful pause and become fully aware of your body's alignment and energy.** Stand or sit up tall with your feet planted firmly, grounding yourself and establishing a strong foundation. Take a deep breath, inhaling self-assurance and exhaling any tension or self-doubt.
2. **Connect with your inner tree.** Visualise yourself as a majestic tree, your body as the solid trunk and your energy extending downward like roots, reaching through the floor into the earth. This imagery reminds you of your grounded strength and power.
3. **Straighten your spine.** Imagine a surge of vitality from the earth travelling up your body to your spine, lengthening and aligning each vertebra. Stand (or sit) tall, as if suspended by invisible strings, and let your spine be a symbol of resilience and presence.
4. **Release shoulder tension.** Focus on your shoulders – those keepers of tension and stress. Roll them back and down a few times, allowing your shoulder blades to glide effortlessly down your back. Embrace the sensation of broadening your chest and opening up to the world. Feel the power radiating through your shoulders, projecting confidence and assertiveness.

5. **Elevate your neck and head.** Shift your awareness to your neck and head. Lift your chin slightly and align your neck with the rest of your spine. Imagine a string is gently pulling the crown of your head upward, elongating your neck and instilling grace.
6. **Open your arms with confidence.** As you stand (or sit) tall and maintain your aligned posture, relax your arms by your sides. Turn your hands so that your palms are facing slightly forward. This welcoming arm position signifies openness and confidence. Breathe deeply. If the situation permits, raise your arms to shoulder height, keeping your palms forward – as if you're about to give a big embrace to all that lies ahead. By adopting this posture, you reinforce a positive self-image and a mindset of self-assuredness, which can boost your confidence and professional presence in any setting.

To take your posture power up to the next level, hit play on an empowering tune. Turn up the volume, rock that confident body language and let the music be the soundtrack to your success. You can find a link to my power-up playlist at lizziewilliamson.com/active.

Mindset move 3: the practice of gratitude

It's a common tendency to focus on what we lack, the challenges we face or what's not going as planned, both personally and professionally. We often find ourselves scrutinising what's missing or what needs improvement. This, along with the occasional frustrations with colleagues or the pressure to meet deadlines, can contribute to a sense of perpetual dissatisfaction and stress.

Gratitude serves as a powerful counterbalance to this natural inclination. It encourages us to shift our focus from what's missing to what's present, from what's wrong to what's right. By intentionally cultivating gratitude, we break free from the confines of a scarcity mindset and embrace the abundance that surrounds us. This change in perspective can be a catalyst for a more positive and fulfilling workday, transforming how we perceive our professional journey and opening the door to greater success and wellbeing. As Alex Korb writes in *The Upward Spiral*, 'there's a gratitude circuit in your brain, badly in need of a workout. Strengthening that circuit brings the power to elevate your physical and mental health, boost happiness, improve sleep, and help you feel more connected to other people'.

Gratitude works its magic on our brains by influencing our neural pathways and chemical reactions. When we practise gratitude regularly, our brains release serotonin and dopamine, neurotransmitters responsible for feelings of pleasure, happiness and motivation. These feel-good chemicals create a positive feedback loop, reinforcing our inclination to focus on the positive aspects of our lives. Over time, this practice strengthens the neural pathways associated with gratitude and positive thinking. It helps us become more attuned to the things that are going well in our lives and less fixated on the negative aspects. As a result, we experience a shift from a negative bias to a more optimistic and grateful outlook.

Why include a gratitude practice in a book about an active workday? Well, optimistic people are more likely to be physically active! In a study on gratitude, participants were divided into three groups, each tasked with writing a few sentences every week with a different focus. The first group wrote about things they were grateful for that had happened that week. The second group wrote about things that had irritated them, while the third group wrote about things that had affected them, without any emphasis on whether they were positive or negative experiences. After ten weeks, those who wrote what they were grateful for reported feeling more optimistic and better about their lives. They also engaged in more physical exercise and had fewer visits to doctors compared to those in the study that focused on what aggravated them.

Practising gratitude in your professional life can be transformative. It's a mindset move that helps you shift your focus away from what's lacking or challenging and redirects it towards the positive aspects of your work and relationships. The impact extends beyond individual wellbeing and reaches the heart of workplace dynamics. Another study discovered that employees who received thanks from their supervisors made a remarkable 50 per cent more fundraising calls compared to their colleagues who didn't receive the same expressions of appreciation. In the context of your state of mind, gratitude can be a potent tool for maintaining a positive and focused outlook in the workplace – even if it feels forced at first!

My morning routine: a journey of gratitude and self-reflection

Let me take you behind the scenes of my everyday morning routine. It's nothing extravagant, just a simple practice that has been my anchor for the past few years, helping me navigate the twists and turns of each day.

I roll out of bed and, almost instinctively, my feet guide me to the window. It's a habit now, like brushing my teeth or brewing a pot of coffee. It may seem like a small moment, but it's become something incredibly special to me. I stand there, in my pyjamas with unruly morning hair, and look outside. This brief moment of serenity marks the beginning of a unique dance between gratitude and self-awareness.

Some mornings, I feel like I've struck gold in the gratitude department. Thoughts flow effortlessly and I find myself thankful for the simplest of things – my family's wellbeing, the comforting embrace of my cosy bed, the work I get to do. These moments of reflection wrap me in a warm cocoon of contentment.

But let's keep it real. Life isn't always a picturesque sunrise and my mornings certainly aren't all sunshine and rainbows. There are days when my well of gratitude feels drier than the Sahara. Maybe life has thrown me some curveballs, or perhaps I'm juggling a hundred thoughts at once. So, there I stand, trying to coax gratitude out of its hiding place, just like I've done countless times before. But it feels like life's worries and stresses have constructed a fortress around it. On those mornings, I've learned not to push it. Instead, I see this as a signal from deep within to check in with my state of mind. It's a sign that it's time to reach into my gratitude toolbox and give my emotions a little nudge in the right direction.

TRY THIS: open your gratitude toolbox

There are various ways to incorporate gratitude into your work, and you can draw inspiration from this gratitude toolbox to find what aligns with your preferences. Try to make gratitude a regular practice by opening your toolbox daily or weekly, ideally at a consistent time so that it becomes a habit. Consider scheduling it in your diary, or seamlessly integrate these tools into specific work situations.

By prioritising your state of mind and taking proactive steps to maintain a positive and focused outlook, you empower yourself to excel in your work, build meaningful connections and navigate the challenges of the workday with resilience and grace. Remember, your state of mind is not just a passive bystander in your professional journey – it's a powerful ally that can lead you to success and fulfillment in your career.

The gratitude flash

As if you were a camera capturing a swift moment of appreciation, take a breath, close your eyes and, in just a few seconds, picture one thing you're grateful for in that very moment. It can be big, or it can be small. In a busy workday, this brief 'flash' allows you to redirect your focus and recognise the positive aspects of your day.

The gratitude spotlight

Amid the sea of papers, screens and devices in your workspace, discover one thing that fills your heart with appreciation – a cherished memento, an inspiring quote or a photo that brings joy. Smile, breathe and let the feelings it gives you expand your heart. Don't have anything that fits the bill? Now's the time to organise something! This gratitude spotlight in your workspace infuses your environment with positivity and serves as a gentle reminder of the good things around you.

The gratitude ripple

Like a pebble gently dropped into a pond, your gratitude ripple begins with a heartfelt thank-you email to a colleague who brightened your day or offered valuable assistance. When you send your words of appreciation, watch how your act of kindness creates ripples of goodwill, fostering a supportive work culture. Not only does it brighten someone else's day, but it also uplifts your own spirits and nurtures a sense of connection within the workplace. Stay tuned for more about culture and connection in the third and final part of this book.

The gratitude tag

Embrace the art of appreciation by leaving gratitude tags throughout your workspace. Like a graffiti artist adorning a wall with inspiring messages, leave sticky notes of gratitude on your computer screen or a colleague's desk. As you spread appreciation, your thoughtful gestures become little tags of inspiration, enhancing the work environment and fostering a sense of camaraderie. These small acts of gratitude can have a significant impact, creating an uplifting atmosphere for everyone around you.

Core points

- Having a positive state of mind is not about being blindly optimistic or suppressing negative emotions. It's about cultivating emotional intelligence and resilience.
- Mindset moves can help you navigate the emotional highway of your workday by helping you feel more optimistic, grateful and connected, and reinvigorating your mind and body.
- One of my favourite mindset moves is to consciously shake your head from side to side while picturing an obligation you're happy to let go of, then nodding your head while imagining a project you're excited to welcome.

- Your body language has a powerful connection to your mindset. Try my posture power-up before your next high-stakes meeting and see how it transforms your confidence.
- Don't forget gratitude – the magic pill for mindset – which has the power to change your mood instantly. What can you feel grateful for today?

8

Take care of your body

Let's get physical

Life is like riding a bicycle. To keep your balance, you must keep moving.

Albert Einstein

It's remarkable how many conversations I've had with people from diverse professional backgrounds – from employees to wellbeing managers to CEOs – who share a common story of the physical pain they endure after a gruelling workweek. They open up to me about the tightness in their shoulders and hips, the stiffness in their necks and their persistent lower-back pain. It's disheartening to hear of the toll that sedentary work takes on their bodies. The hours spent sitting without proper breaks and movement wreak havoc on their muscles and hinder blood circulation, leading to discomfort and pain.

It's not just the time spent sitting that causes their agony; it's also the *way* they sit. They spend hours upon hours with their bodies seemingly frozen, stuck in the same position. Whether it's hunching over a document, staring at a computer screen or perpetually craning their neck to look at their smartphone, they remain in a prolonged state of immobility. It's no wonder their bodies rebel against their confinement. And then there are the repetitive tasks they face day in and day out: the endless typing, clicking, writing and scrolling only intensify the problem. Overworked muscles become tight and fatigued, while others are left underutilised, resulting in imbalances, weakness and further discomfort.

When we have these conversations, it becomes apparent that in the pursuit of meeting deadlines and being productive, they sacrifice the moments of movement their bodies so desperately need. They cast aside the opportunity to stretch, move and reset – and they're facing the consequences.

When the COVID-19 pandemic hit and remote work became the new norm, many of us found ourselves with less-than-ideal work set-ups and without the incidental prompts to get up and move that we had at the office. With many of us on back-to-back virtual meetings, we were perched on kitchen chairs, slouched on couches and hunched over laptops for hours on end. A staggering 70 per cent of all respondents to an Employees Working From Home study experienced musculoskeletal pain or discomfort due to their remote set-up, while another survey reported a notable increase of 30 per cent in musculoskeletal injuries. The most prevalent issues reported were back, shoulder and neck pain.

It doesn't matter whether you're working from home or the office – not paying attention to your body's needs while sitting at your desk can cause a whole bunch of problems. Prolonged sitting without movement can cause a substantial increase in stiffness of the back muscles, heightening the risk of lower back pain. While this discomfort might seem bearable in the short term, over time it can lead to muscles becoming progressively tighter and weaker, and it may even contribute to misalignment in your spine. Believe me, chronic pain and restricted mobility aren't the ingredients for an enjoyable work experience.

It's not just about the aches and pains, either. Prolonged sitting can mess with circulation, digestion and lung capacity, and even make us feel tired and unfocused. Our bodies are meant to move, and sitting for hours on end can wreak havoc on our overall health. That's why study after study recommends breaking up long hours of sitting with movement.

You know what brings me joy? It's hearing from professionals after they've started incorporating micro moves into their workday. The aches and pains gradually subside and they discover the power they have to reclaim their physical wellbeing, even within the confines of their work environment.

Beyond the physical: strengthening for career resilience

I'd like to introduce you to Roxanne. Her story of professional reinvention stands out as a testament to the power of movement. Roxanne's journey begins with a twist of fate – a job loss that struck her like a bolt of lightning in the middle of her career.

After dedicating years to a role she had cherished, often at the expense of her wellbeing, Roxanne found herself standing at a crossroads with her confidence in tatters. The loss of her job was a blow to her ego and she was navigating the treacherous waters of job hunting with a heavy heart. The market had transformed since she was last looking for a job, and algorithms seemed to dictate the fate of her CV and applications without so much as a glance from a human.

As Roxanne's pursuit of employment consumed her, she put her personal wellbeing on the backburner and focused solely on securing her next paycheque. Fortunately, perseverance led her to a new job opportunity that promised a fresh start and financial stability. However, it came with the challenge of adapting to a new industry and role, a burden that took a toll on her physical and mental health.

Around three months into her new job, Roxanne had an awakening. While her professional life seemed to be back on track, something was amiss. She could feel the strain of a sedentary lifestyle creeping into her muscles and her back ached from hours of sitting. It dawned on her that she had been neglecting her own needs, prioritising everyone else in her work and household above herself.

Determined to make a change, Roxanne made a commitment to herself:

> *Working from home, I began incorporating short bursts of physical activity into my day, whether it was five minutes of weights, squats or a walking meeting. I even let my colleagues know that I was walking during meetings to boost efficiency. I wanted to make it clear that I wasn't slacking off; I was investing in my wellbeing to become a better, more productive worker. I refuse to let age or circumstances define my future. I aim to enter my fifties as a fit, agile and content person, setting an example for my daughters and proving that taking care of yourself is essential, no matter your role or responsibilities.*

Incorporating movement into her daily work routine, Roxanne uncovered confidence and resilience. She became proof that prioritising physical health doesn't just invigorate the body but also fortifies the mind. With her body and mind in harmony, Roxanne is thriving in her career, emerging as a role model not only for her daughters but for everyone who crosses her path.

Micro moves, macro impact

So, let me ask you: have you ever experienced that strain, that nagging ache in your body after a long day or week of work? If you have, it's time for you to embrace body boosts and prioritise taking care of your body.

You are well aware by now of the remarkable impact of bringing more movement into your routine, leading to a noticeable reduction in musculoskeletal discomfort associated with sedentary work lifestyles. It's time to give that precious body of yours more mobility, flexibility and strength with these three essential body boosts – micro moves with maximum impact. Think of these micro moves as mini love letters to your body – little reminders that you value and prioritise your physical health. Trust me, your body will appreciate it and you'll reap the benefits.

Micro move 1: your solution to sitting woes

Simply sitting less is often suggested as a remedy for prolonged sitting, but let's be honest – in the reality of your busy workday, it's easier said than done. Your job may require you to spend significant hours at your desk glued to your computer, and taking frequent breaks may not always be feasible. Or maybe, if you have a device that alerts you when it's time to move, you always seem to be in the middle of something important and don't want to stop.

You might be thinking, *There's no way I can find time to step away from my chair and move. I'm caught up in back-to-back meetings and feel chained to my desk.* If this is you, don't worry! An active workday isn't just about sitting less; it's also about moving more, with studies showing that even the smallest of moves done in your chair can make a difference.

Let's shift your perspective on that chair of yours. It's not just a static piece of furniture; it's a gateway to a world of invigorating possibilities. Instead of seeing it as a constraint, consider it your launchpad to a more dynamic and energised work experience. Your chair can be the catalyst for exercises that take care of your body, awaken your muscles and infuse your day with renewed vitality.

Research indicates that even small movements performed while seated can have a positive impact. By taking just a few minutes – or seconds! – throughout your workday to perform simple movements, you can proactively combat the negative consequences of prolonged sitting and make your chair a friendlier place for your back.

You discovered some sneaky chair moves with the undercover chairercise in chapter 2. Allow me to introduce you to another micro move that will revolutionise how you view your chair forever.

TRY THIS: dynamic sitting moves

Dynamic sitting moves are exercises are designed to mobilise your lower back, maintain flexibility and prevent stiffness from setting in, ensuring you maintain a healthy and comfortable posture. Think of them as a mini-investment in your wellbeing. Instead of waiting for the discomfort and pain to creep in, you're taking proactive steps to keep your back happy and healthy, right from your desk. You may have heard the famous quote by the inventor of the Pilates method, Joseph Pilates: 'If your spine is inflexibly stiff at 30, you are old. If it is completely flexible at 60, you are young.'

These dynamic sitting moves are your secret weapon against the perils of prolonged sitting, no matter how busy your workday. As you sit at your desk, working away, take a moment to let your spine twist, your torso lean and your body rock and roll. Every hour, try doing four to eight of each move, either choosing just one or two at a time or doing all four in a row. Feel the rejuvenation and release of tension as you restore mobility, maintain flexibility and prevent stiffness from setting in – especially in your lower back.

Spine twist

Feel the rejuvenating twist in your spine as you rotate your torso to the left, allowing both shoulders to gracefully follow. Then, unwind and twist your torso to the right, letting your shoulders mirror the movement. Experience the gentle release of tension as you restore mobility to your spine, particularly in the lower back.

Spine tilt

Keeping your buttocks planted in the chair, engage your core and lean your body to the left, simultaneously lifting your right shoulder towards the sky. Feel the stretch and lengthening along the right side of your torso. Transition to the other side by tilting your body to the right and lifting your left shoulder. This movement enhances flexibility and encourages a balanced spine, especially in the lumbar region.

Spine rock

Gently tilt your pelvis forward, creating a subtle rounding in your lower back. Allow your spine to release and relax in this position and your shoulders to do the same. Next, shift your pelvis backward, creating a gentle arch in your lower back and elongating your spine.

Alternate between these two fluid movements, nurturing your lower back and promoting flexibility in your spine.

Spine roll

We're going to add some rockin' to your roll. Lean your body slightly forward with a straight back and engage in a gentle clockwise motion, allowing your upper body to roll to the right, back, left and front again. Imagine drawing a perfect circle with your upper body in a seamless flow of movement. Engage your core muscles and continue in this direction until you are ready to change to an anticlockwise motion. This nourishing move helps keep your spine supple and your core engaged, particularly focusing on your lower back and hip flexors.

Micro move 2: bye-bye tension

'Your body is a reflection of your lifestyle' is a statement that holds profound wisdom. Our bodies are remarkable creations, capable of incredible feats of resilience, but they're also mirrors of how we treat them. In the world of modern work, where hours blur into one another and screens demand our unwavering attention, it's easy to neglect our bodies. We sit, we type and we stare at our screens, often forgetting that our bodies long for movement, flexibility and release.

Picture this. You're deep into a work project, deadline looming, and discomfort begins to seep into your body. Maybe it's a nagging stiffness in your neck, a dull ache in your shoulders and hips or a persistent twinge in your lower back. Muscle tightness has crashed the party and, as we do too often, you allow it to linger. Of course, you have work to complete, so you soldier on.

But here's the thing: your body's tightening muscles are trying to send you a message, saying, 'Hey, I need some attention here!' Ignoring this message can have consequences. Tight muscles not only lead to discomfort but can also limit your range of motion, affect your posture and even lead to chronic pain. The longer we sit in the same position, the more our muscles tighten and the more we compromise our body's flexibility.

Now, imagine a different scenario. You're still deeply engrossed in your work, but this time, as that familiar tightness creeps in, you address it. The discomfort may be similar, but your response is different. You recognise that your body is sending you signals – much like the cue element of the habit loop I described in chapter 4 – that should not be ignored. You reach into your active workday toolkit for a quick stretch, a simple routine you've woven into your workday with no need for a yoga mat or activewear.

With each deliberate stretch, you send a clear message to your body: *I'm here for you*. The practice isn't just about momentary relief, either. It's a strategic move to maintain your body's flexibility, relieve tension and promote overall wellbeing. This little moment becomes your trusted ally, ensuring that muscle tightness doesn't linger and discomfort doesn't compromise your workday.

There are a number of reasons for getting more flexible at work. Flexibility is the key to unlocking your body's full range of motion. It's like oiling the hinges of a rusty door, allowing it to swing open freely. With increased flexibility, you can reach, bend and twist with ease in both work and daily life.

Tight muscles often pull your body out of alignment, leading to poor posture. Regular stretching helps realign your body, promoting a more upright and confident stance. You'll find yourself sitting and standing taller, exuding self-assuredness. Flexible muscles and tendons are also less prone to injury. By incorporating stretching into your routine, you're providing your body with a shield against strains, sprains and other work-related injuries. For those already grappling with discomfort or pain, regular stretching can be a game-changer. It releases tension and soothes sore muscles, and can be an effective tool in managing chronic pain.

Finally, the act of stretching isn't just physical; it's a mental reset too. When you stretch, you focus on your body and your breath, momentarily disconnecting from the demands of work. Just like the brain-boosting micro moves I shared with you in chapter 6, you can also use stretching as a mini meditation to reduce stress and enhance mental clarity. By taking these proactive measures, you're not only preventing immediate discomfort but also safeguarding your long-term physical health and enhancing your productivity.

TRY THIS: all aboard the stretch express

It's time to take a ride on the stretch express. Get your ticket to a more comfortable and vibrant work experience, where your body's wellbeing is a priority and discomfort is shown the door.

Boarding the stretch express is simpler than you might think. Here are a series of micro-stretches designed to target those common tightness hotspots – the neck, shoulders, hips, hamstrings and lower back. These stretches can be seamlessly woven into your workday, giving you a quick dose of tension relief without you ever leaving your desk. Picture yourself embracing each stretch as a small act of self-care, a moment of mindfulness amid the chaos of your workday.

Neck and shoulders

You know when your neck starts to ache or your shoulders feel all tense? Yep, blame it on sitting for hours with poor posture and craning your neck forward. It's a common issue, especially if you're working at a desk and staring at a screen.

Try taking your left arm up and over your head so your hand ends up over your right ear. Gently guide your left ear towards your left shoulder, keeping your right shoulder down. Hold for two to four breaths and then repeat on the other side. Feel the tension melt away as you release the tightness in your neck and shoulder muscles.

Upper body

Working for long hours in the same position can leave your upper body feeling stuck and restricted. The static posture and repetitive movements associated with desk work can take a toll, causing discomfort and limiting your range of motion. But fear not; there's a simple exercise that can help you break free from that confined state and restore flexibility to your upper body.

Extend your arms in front of you and clasp your hands together. As you look towards your toes, imagine someone gently pulling your hands forward. Simultaneously, initiate a slow and controlled backward movement, allowing your spine to arch gently. Feel the delightful stretch as your upper back and shoulders open up. Maintain a relaxed and comfortable breath as you hold this position for a few seconds.

Lower back

Oh boy, sitting for too long can really put a strain on your lower back. It's no surprise that many of us experience nagging pain or stiffness in that area. This seated spinal twist provides a soothing stretch for your lower back and helps improve its flexibility.

Sit tall in your chair and cross one leg over the other. Gently twist your torso towards the crossed leg, using the armrest or back of the chair to help if needed. With each inhalation, lengthen your spine, and with each exhalation, deepen the twist. Take two to four breaths in this twisted position, feeling the release of tension in your lower back and the improved mobility in your spine. Repeat the exercise on the other side.

Hips, hamstrings and knees

After hours of sitting, it's common to notice discomfort in your hips, hamstrings and knees. Prolonged periods of sitting can disrupt blood circulation and cause tightness in your muscles, leaving you feeling achy and stiff. Your hip flexors and knees may not be too happy about being in a bent position for hours on end, but there's a simple exercise that can help you relieve tension and bring flexibility to your lower body.

Begin by lifting your right foot slightly off the ground. Then, with a gentle motion, extend that leg out in front of you so your leg is straight and your heel is on the floor. (You may have to sit further forward on your chair.) As you do so, bring your toes back towards yourself, intensifying the stretch in the back of your legs and targeting your hamstrings. To deepen the stretch, lift your torso and lean slightly forward. Hold for two to ten breaths, then bring your right foot back to the starting position and repeat with your other leg. Embrace the opportunity to create space and openness in your lower body as you perform this stretch.

Micro move 3: office strength essentials

In today's predominantly desk-bound work culture, we can find ourselves glued to chairs and screens for hours on end. Unfortunately, this seemingly harmless habit can take a toll on our strength.

When you sit for extended periods, your muscles become dormant. They're like sleepy sentinels, disengaged and waiting for action. Over time, this inactivity can lead to muscle imbalance and weakness, particularly in the muscles that support your spine and maintain posture. Imagine those back muscles you need when lifting a heavy object getting rusty from lack of use. The hip flexors, essential for stability and balance, are also silently protesting as they remain in a contracted position while you sit. This weakening of crucial muscle groups can make you more susceptible to strains and injuries when you finally do engage in physical activities, whether it's lifting a box or bending down to tie your shoe.

So, what is there to do about this sapping of strength? The answer lies in getting strong. The journey to strength isn't merely a short-term endeavour; it's a lifelong investment in your health. A strong body is equipped to ward off various chronic conditions that can arise with age. By maintaining your strength, you're actively lowering your risk of heart disease, diabetes, osteoporosis and more. The strength you build today becomes a protective shield for your body's future, contributing to a healthier and more fulfilling life for years to come.

Recent research, highlighted in meta-analysis published in the *British Journal of Sports Medicine*, underscores the long-term benefits of muscle-strengthening workouts and emphasises the importance of taking care of your body through strength exercises. The comprehensive study found that individuals who incorporate muscle-strengthening exercises into their routine are less likely to experience premature mortality compared to those who neglect such workouts.

Preventing work-related injuries isn't just about luck; it's about being proactive. Strength training is your steadfast ally in this endeavour. By building muscular strength, enhancing joint stability and promoting balanced muscle development, you're investing in a safer, more resilient work life. With better body mechanics, increased bone density and the confidence to tackle any challenge, you're well on your way to a healthier, injury-free tomorrow.

Remarkably, even a relatively modest commitment of just 30 to 60 minutes a week of strength training yields substantial health advantages. When you break it down, that's only a few minutes each day! And the good news is that muscle-strengthening exercises don't have to resemble a traditional gym workout that demands an hour of strenuous activity with specialised equipment. It's time to turn your office into your very own personal strength sanctuary.

TRY THIS: muscle strengthening solutions

If you can't get to a gym – or even if you can! – the solution is to incorporate regular micro strengthening moves into your workday. Small strengthening moves each day can actually be more beneficial than one or two big training sessions in your week, according to one study. These simple exercises are antidotes to the sedentary curse. They not only wake up your muscles but also provide a refreshing break from the monotony of sitting.

Working on your muscles has not only physical but also emotional benefits. In *The Joy of Movement: How exercise helps us find happiness, hope, connection, and courage* Kelly McGonigal writes, 'Every time we move our muscles, we are giving ourselves an intravenous dose of hope'. When your muscles contract, they release mood-enhancing chemicals into your bloodstream, including myokines, which are often called 'hope molecules'. Myokines not only increase muscle strength but also make you feel more resilient.

When you're waiting for a report to load or a meeting to start, why not squeeze in a wall squat or a few heel raises? It's a win-win situation – you're boosting your strength and breaking the cycle of prolonged sitting. Strength training isn't just about pumping iron at the gym; it's about embracing a lifestyle that values the resilience of your body and mind, especially in the face of sedentary work habits. By making these micro-strength moves a regular part of your workday, you're taking a stand against the adverse effects of prolonged sitting, ensuring that your body remains strong, agile and ready for whatever challenges your work throws your way.

Kitchen bench and wall push-ups

Push-ups are a powerful way to boost your mental and physical wellbeing, and you don't need a gym or plenty of space to do them. Let's explore two variations that can leave you with a profound sense of strength and empowerment.

First we have kitchen bench push-ups. This is a gentle yet empowering variation of push-ups to enhance your physical and mental strength. Kitchen bench push-ups are the perfect micro move for when you're waiting for the kettle to boil, on the way back from the bathroom or on your lunchbreak:

1. Stand facing a sturdy kitchen bench or countertop.
2. Place your hands slightly wider than shoulder-width apart on the edge of the bench or countertop.
3. Step back to create a plank position, ensuring your body forms a straight line from head to heels.
4. Lower your chest towards the bench while engaging your core, bending your elbows to wherever feels comfortable.
5. Push back up to the starting position, using your arm and chest muscles.
6. Repeat as many times as you can in two minutes.

The second variation is wall push-ups. These are great for elevating your energy levels and boosting mental clarity. Good times to do wall push-ups include before a meeting to boost alertness, after a long period of sitting to re-energise and whenever you feel like a quick mental and physical reset:

1. Stand facing a sturdy wall, about arm's-length away.
2. Place your palms on the wall at shoulder height, shoulder-width apart to create a plank position.
3. Lean your body towards the wall, bending your elbows to bring your chest closer.
4. Push back to the starting position, engaging your core and arm muscles.
5. Repeat the movement ten to 20 times or many times as feels comfortable.

Heel raises

Heel raises are discreet yet effective exercises for enhancing calf muscles and lower-leg stability. This micro move is ideal for nurturing lower-body strength, even within the confines of your workspace. Try doing heel raises while waiting for a document to print, during a phone call or video conference and when waiting in a queue:

1. Stand with your feet hip-width apart.
2. Raise your heels off the ground, lifting through the balls of your feet.
3. Hold the raised position for a moment, engaging your calf muscles.
4. Gently lower your heels back to the ground.
5. Repeat as many times as is comfortable for you.

Wall squats

Wall squats provide an excellent opportunity to bolster lower body strength and stability. These exercises engage such key muscle groups as your quadriceps, hamstrings and glutes, all while allowing you to stay productive at work. Wall squats are great for when you're waiting for a colleague in a meeting room, a file to download or the kettle to boil:

1. Stand with your back against a wall, feet hip-width apart.
2. Slowly slide down the wall, inching your feet out as you go and bending your knees as if sitting in an imaginary chair.

3. Lower yourself until your thighs are parallel to the ground (or higher if that's too challenging), all while maintaining contact with the wall and ensuring that your knees don't go over your toes.
4. Maintain this position for as many seconds as you can, focusing on engaging your leg muscles.
5. Gradually rise back up to the starting position by inching your feet back in and carefully straightening your knees.

Chair core crunch

Core strength is pivotal for maintaining stability and posture throughout your workday. The core-engaging desk plank is a micro move that targets your core muscles, enhancing abdominal strength and overall core stability. Having a strong core isn't just about showing off a six-pack; it's about caring for the intricate network of muscles that stabilises your spine and pelvis. It plays a crucial role in maintaining good posture, preventing back pain and supporting your overall physical wellbeing.

In a busy workday, getting down on the floor for a set of traditional crunches might not be a feasible option. However, this doesn't mean you have to neglect your core. There is no need to leave your chair; simply lean back, engage those abdominal muscles and reclaim your core strength with the chair core crunch. Ideas for when you can do chair core crunches include when you're listening to someone on the phone, between meetings and before getting up for lunch:

1. Sit up straight towards the front of your chair.
2. Place your hands on the top of your thighs, palms down, fingers pointing towards your knees.
3. Take a deep breath in and engage your abdominal muscles.
4. Tuck your hips under to protect your lower back.
5. Lean back slightly while maintaining a control of the movement.
6. Feel the tension in your core as you hold for a moment.

7. Breathe out and return to an upright sitting position by bringing your body forward, using your abdominal muscles to guide the movement.
8. Repeat this movement ten to 20 times, or as many times as is comfortable for you.

Core points

- Whether you work in an office or from home, not paying attention to your body's needs while sitting at your desk can cause problems.
- People are conditioned to overlook their body's needs, whether that's rest, nourishment or movement. How can you listen to your body more closely? During the workday, what is it crying out for?
- Even if your job demands long hours in the chair, there are ways to sit more freely.
- Research indicates that even small movements performed while seated can have a positive impact.
- Try incorporating regular stretching breaks into your workday. It can be amazing how different you feel after just a week. Don't just trust me – try it!

9

Improve your mood

Rediscovering your best self

Be ~~with~~ someone who makes you happy.

Mel Robbins

So, you're not in a good mood at work today. Maybe you woke up on the wrong side of the bed or something in your personal life is weighing on your mind. It happens to all of us – we're only human. It's natural, we all have those days. But have you ever wondered how your mood affects your workday and overall experience in the workplace?

Your mood plays a crucial role in shaping your work life – and its influence is probably far greater than you think. It influences your productivity, workplace interactions and even overall job satisfaction. When you're in a positive and joyful mood, tasks seem more manageable and challenges become opportunities to shine. On the other hand, when you're feeling down or stressed, work can feel like an uphill battle and your enthusiasm may dwindle.

Moreover, your mood can influence how you interact with colleagues and clients. If you're feeling irritable or low, it might affect your communication and collaboration, potentially leading to misunderstandings or conflicts. Your colleagues may also notice the change in your demeanour, impacting the overall team dynamic.

It's not all doom and gloom. Recognising your mood and its potential impact is the first step towards turning things around. Enter the transformative power of mood-boosting micro moves – short moments of intentional movement to shake off stress and let go of what's weighing you down.

From dreary to cheery: the power of movement

Picture this. You get to work feeling low, struggling to find the energy to face the day. The weight of your low mood seems to have a gravitational pull, making it challenging to begin your to-do list. As you trudge through your work tasks, your mind feels foggy and time seems to slow down. Interacting with colleagues becomes daunting and laughter feels like a distant memory.

Now, envision an alternative scenario. Despite starting work with a low mood, you decide to take a small step to improve your day. You engage in movement, whether through a short walk, stretching exercises or dancing to your favourite song. As you move, you feel a spark of energy and a faint smile emerges. The chemicals in your body begin to shift and a glimmer of hope brightens your outlook.

Movement has a profound impact on our mood. When we engage in physical activity, our body releases neurotransmitters endorphins, dopamine and serotonin – 'happiness chemicals' that play a vital role in reducing stress, boosting mood and promoting overall wellbeing. Essentially, movement is a way to return to the present moment and let go of distractions and worries that cloud the mind during moments of overwhelm.

The paradox of movement is that it can be hard to motivate ourselves to engage in it when we don't feel good. Though the initial resistance might feel overwhelming, acknowledging this resistance as a sign that we need it more than ever can be empowering. So too can be turning an all-or-nothing mindset into an all-or something approach, because something is so much better than nothing. Remember the story I told you at the start of chapter 2, when I was trying for just a single plié at my kitchen bench? Taking that first step, no matter how small, opens a positive feedback loop in which movement begets an improved mood, which in turn motivates us to continue moving.

Mood-boosting micro moves are simple yet powerful moments of happiness we intentionally incorporate into our workday. These boosts don't have to be time-consuming or elaborate; they can be as short as just a few minutes. The key is that they are activities that not only spark joy but also interrupt the spiralling of negative emotions.

As you incorporate micro moves into your active workday, you'll find that happiness can be found in even the tiniest moments, creating a ripple effect in both your professional life and your personal life. So, let's embark on the journey of taking breaks for mood-enhancing micro moves, one small moment at a time.

Why bother with mood-boosting micro moves?

The first and most obvious reason to take a micro move from your toolkit during your workday is the instant effect of mood elevation they deliver. Whether it's a shadow box or a moment to 'shake it off', the rush of endorphins can bring joy and positivity to your day. It's also an excellent stress reliever. When you take a moment to move, your body releases tension and your mind finds temporary relief from work-related pressures. This stress reduction allows room for joy to enter and brighten your workday.

Feeling drained and low on energy during the workday? Movement can provide a much-needed energy boost. Moving your body increases blood flow and oxygen levels, revitalising your mind and body for increased focus and productivity. It can also become a form of mindfulness in action. As you engage in intentional movements, you become fully present in the moment, letting go of distractions and worries. This mindful immersion in movement opens the door to experiencing joy in the here and now. Amid repetitive tasks and routines, movement offers a refreshing break from monotony. A short dance break or a walk around the office can inject moments of joy and playfulness into your workday.

Finally, movement is fun! Movement allows for creative self-expression. Whether it's through dancing, stretching or other physical activities, you can tap into your creativity and experience joy in the process of self-discovery. Adding moments of mood-boosting movement to your workday breaks the seriousness of work tasks and allows you to enjoy the work journey, rather than just focusing on the end goal.

Mood boost 1: letting go and thriving

It's natural to be affected by negative encounters at work. The key to thriving in the face of these challenges lies in our ability to let go and move forward. Negative thoughts and feelings can be a heavy burden, slowing us down and impacting our workday in various ways.

Imagine carrying a backpack filled with stones weighing you down as you navigate through your day. Each negative thought or annoyance adds another stone to that backpack, making it harder to walk with ease and focus on the tasks at hand. The weight of these emotions can drain your mental and emotional energy, making you feel overwhelmed and distracted.

Learning how to let go and embrace emotional resilience in your workday is a powerful advantage. By using tools and techniques to release negativity and move on, you lighten that backpack and free yourself of unnecessary burdens. You create space for emotional wellbeing, allowing you to focus on what truly matters – your work, your goals and your growth.

This is not about suppressing or denying your emotions; it's about acknowledging, processing and then releasing them. It's like recognising the stones in your backpack, feeling their weight and deciding to put them down one by one.

TRY THIS: shake and shadow-box it off

If you're a Swiftie like me, you know that Taylor Swift's 'Shake It Off' is more than just a catchy song – it's a mantra for bouncing back from negativity and embracing a positive outlook.

It's not uncommon to encounter moments of annoyance and frustration at work. Whether they're caused by a problematic colleague, a setback on a project or a never-ending to-do list, these moments can leave us feeling weighed down and overwhelmed. In embracing the spirit of 'Shake It Off' in your workday, however, you can shake away those feelings of annoyance and frustration to find liberation and renewed energy. This can be a game-changer, helping you maintain focus, productivity and a happier state of mind.

Next time you feel annoyance or frustration creeping in at work, shake and shadow-box it off with this simple exercise:

1. Step away from your workspace to find a private spot to move freely without feeling self-conscious. I've heard from many people who do moves like this in the bathroom!
2. Inhale deeply, and as you exhale begin to visualise letting go of tension or negative energy and let your body soften.
3. Begin by gently shaking your hands, then your arms, and gradually move to your shoulders and upper body. Let the shaking spread down to your legs and feet. Shake it all slowly or quickly, whatever feels comfortable for your joints, releasing any pent-up frustration or annoyance.
4. Now start shadow boxing. Position your feet shoulder-width apart, knees slightly bent, and form relaxed, loose fists while visualising stress sources ahead. Start gentle air punches with controlled movements, engaging core muscles and pivoting torso and hips for added punch movement.
5. If you want more, add some kicks to the front and side to kick away that stress.
6. Embrace the release. As you shake and punch, imagine letting go of everything bothering you. Feel the weight of your dark mood lifting off your shoulders and moving through and out of your body.
7. Continue for as long as you need!

A personal story: addressing emotions head on

In the fast-paced world of work, it's easy to overlook our emotional wellbeing and push ourselves to the limit. But I've learned that acknowledging and addressing my emotions head-on can be a game-changer.

I vividly recall a challenging workday when I felt like my emotions were on a rollercoaster, threatening to derail my composure and productivity. It was a day filled with tight deadlines, unexpected obstacles and constant demands. On top of that, I had personal worries that were getting me down.

The stress and frustration built up inside me like a pressure cooker as I sat at my desk. I felt overwhelmed and on the verge of bursting, just like I had felt during those early parenting years. This time, however, I remembered a lesson I had learned from my journey as a parent: denying or suppressing emotions isn't a healthy strategy. I would need to acknowledge and process what I was feeling.

In that moment, I decided to take a break for a mood-boosting micro move. I stood up from my desk and started punching and kicking the air with controlled movements. With each punch and each kick, I felt a sense of release, as if I was unloading the weight of the day. I noticed my emotions starting to shift. The intensity of the stress began to subside, and clarity and calm began to emerge. It wasn't a magic fix and the stress didn't vanish entirely, but I felt more balanced and composed. Returning to my desk, I had transformed the emotional storm into a manageable wave. I wasn't bottling up my feelings or letting them simmer until they exploded; instead, I was honouring my emotions and giving them the attention they deserved.

From that day on, mood-boosting micro moves became my go-to strategy during challenging workdays. Whenever I felt overwhelmed, stressed or uncertain, I would take a few moments to move my body – whether it was shadow-boxing, stretching or taking a brisk walk. Each time, these intentional breaks helped me release tension, regain focus and approach my tasks with a clearer perspective.

Mood boost 2: cultivating boundaries with chair yoga

The boundary between your work and personal lives can easily blur. There might be something going on at home that has a negative effect on your mood, such as family issues or other personal concerns, and that can be a heavy companion when you step into your workday. It can cast a shadow on your productivity and interactions with colleagues. What's even more challenging is that this mood often refuses to stay behind when you clock out, making it challenging to fully engage with the people and activities that bring you joy. This constant juggling can take a toll on your mood, leaving you feeling frazzled and overwhelmed.

Yoga is a holistic solution to this dilemma. It demonstrates that improving your mood doesn't necessarily entail vigorous activities that can often feel too challenging when starting from a low base. Rather, it's a subtle yet powerful approach to improving your mood. This practice releases the tension, anxiety and stress that accumulates during your workday, even if you hadn't realised you'd been carrying those feelings. It offers a mindful opportunity to let go of the burdens you brought to work and leave behind any that you've accumulated during the day as you transition into your personal life.

Studies consistently show that practices such as yoga not only promote and improve respiratory and cardiovascular function but also significantly reduce stress, anxiety, depression and chronic pain. They can help improve sleep patterns and enhance your overall wellbeing, ultimately contributing to a more positive and balanced emotional state.

So, what if you're not able to transform your office into a makeshift yoga studio complete with space for downward-facing dog or tree pose? Introducing chair yoga! At its core, chair yoga is a daily ritual that helps you find your centre right at your desk, regardless of the chaos that might surround you. It doesn't require a special space or equipment – just your chair and yourself. Through its stretches and poses, it invites you to take deep breaths, release the burdens of the day and focus on the present moment – the sensations in your body, the rhythm of your breath and the stillness within.

As you unroll your metaphorical yoga mat – that is, sit at your trusty chair – and cycle through the following five poses, remember that chair yoga isn't just about physical wellbeing; it's a mindful practice for the beginning or end of your workday that can boost your mood by helping you create boundaries between work and home life. It's your sanctuary for a more balanced, centred and connected existence, allowing you to embrace each moment with authenticity and presence. Chair yoga, in its quiet simplicity, provides the space you need to recentre yourself and improve your mood so you can face the world with a sense of calm and clarity.

TRY THIS: your chair yoga cheat sheet

Here are five poses you can flow through at your chair at the end of the workday. With gentle movements and purposeful breaths, each stretch becomes a symbol of release, as if you're shedding the weight of the day and making room for the peace that awaits.

Seated forward bend

Inhale deeply, lengthen your spine, and as you exhale hinge at your hips to gently fold forward. Let your head hang heavy, allowing your neck and shoulders to release. Take a few breaths here, feeling the stretch in your shoulders and lower back, then slowly roll back up.

Seated spinal twist

Inhale and sit tall, then exhale as you twist gently to the right, placing your left hand on your right knee and your right hand on the back of the chair. Inhale again to lengthen your spine, and as you exhale deepen the twist. Feel the gentle rotation in your spine and the release of tension in your lower back. Repeat on the other side.

Eagle arm stretch

Begin by raising both arms to shoulder height. Cross your right arm over the left, intertwining the forearms and pressing palms together if possible (or pressing the backs of your hands together if not). Lift the elbows slightly and relax your shoulders away from your ears. Hold the stretch, feeling the release across your upper back and shoulders. Then switch, repeating the stretch with the left arm over the right. Breathe deeply and allow your body to relax into the stretch, avoiding any discomfort.

Seated warrior pose

Inhale deeply, raising both arms towards the ceiling, elongating the spine. Then exhale, lowering the arms to shoulder height out to the side, palms facing down. Turn your head to gently gaze at your right fingertips, relax your shoulders and breathe steadily. This focus on your fingers encourages present-moment awareness. Hold for a few breaths, then return to the centre and repeat on the other side

Seated cat-cow

Inhale, arch your back and lift your chest as you look up towards the ceiling, with your hands on your knees. Exhale, round your back and tuck your chin towards your chest. Flow through these movements with your breath, massaging your spine and promoting flexibility.

As you conclude your chair yoga session, take a moment to reflect on how you feel. Notice the sense of calmness that has washed over you. You've created a boundary, a space of transition and a moment of closure. The stresses of the day no longer have a hold on you. You're now ready to step into your personal time with a restored body and a clear mind, better able to connect with those most important to you.

Core points

- Movement has a profound impact on mood – and mood influences productivity, workplace interactions and overall job satisfaction.

- Mood-boosting micro moves are simple yet powerful moments of happiness you can intentionally incorporate into your workday. They not only spark joy but also interrupt the spiralling effect of negative emotions.
- Create work–life boundaries with the gentle power of chair yoga – a series of five poses you can do from your chair without even changing into yoga pants. I dare you to try it.
- Movement can become a form of mindfulness in action. As you engage in intentional movements, you become fully present in the moment, letting go of distractions and worries.
- As you incorporate micro moves into your active workday, you'll find that happiness can be found in even the tiniest moments, creating a ripple effect in both your professional life and your personal life.

10

Vitalise your energy

Rekindle the flame within

Without passion, you don't have energy. Without energy, you have nothing.

Warren Buffett

Energy is a prized commodity, a vital force that propels us through the ever-evolving landscape of work, personal aspirations and daily responsibilities. Yet, despite the growing emphasis on self-care and wellbeing, a significant number of people find themselves grappling with a pervasive energy crisis.

Consider for a moment how often you've heard or uttered any of these phrases:

- 'I'm so tired all the time.'
- 'I can't seem to focus anymore.'
- 'I'm emotionally drained.'
- 'I wish I had more energy.'

These sentiments resonate deeply with many individuals, and there's a shared understanding of the daily struggle to maintain energy levels.

The consequences of energy depletion ripple through every facet of our lives. When our energy wanes, our wellbeing and performance suffer. Fatigue sets in, turning routine activities into exhausting endeavours. Lack of physical energy can lead to a sedentary lifestyle, muscle weakness and overall diminished health. Cognitive functions falter and even basic decision-making becomes arduous. Mental fatigue can hinder creativity, problem-solving and the ability to focus on tasks. Emotional resilience dwindles, making it challenging to manage stress, navigate conflicts and maintain a positive outlook. Emotional exhaustion can lead to strained relationships and a reduced quality of life.

Fatigue isn't just a personal concern; it poses workplace hazards that can jeopardise health and safety. Fatigue resulting from prolonged mental or physical exertion can impair performance and mental alertness, leading to potentially dangerous errors. The consequences include decreased motivation, slower reaction times, reduced alertness, compromised concentration, memory and information-processing difficulties, and impaired judgement. A US study revealed that worker fatigue cost employers a staggering US$136.4 billion in health-related lost productive time.

The repercussions of energy depletion are far-reaching, affecting our personal lives, careers and overall wellbeing. It's a challenge that demands our attention and its effects must be combated with proactive measures.

The promise of energy renewal: the spark

What if there was a way to break free from this cycle? What if you could tap into the hidden reservoirs of energy that lie dormant within you, ready to be awakened? By now, you've probably guessed how to get to that source of energy – through physical activity! There's a profound connection between physical movement and energy. Engaging your body in movement doesn't drain your energy; rather, it multiplies it, granting you access to your inner reservoir of vitality. It's time to dispel the myth that physical activity makes you more tired.

When you partake in cardiovascular activities (including those you're about to discover), your heart rate quickens, oxygen courses through your veins and your body releases endorphins – the body's natural energisers. This surge of biochemical activity isn't a drain on your energy; it fuels your day. The increased blood flow and oxygen supply nourish your brain, sharpening your cognitive faculties and enhancing your focus.

So, with that myth out the way, let's turn to a quick lesson in chemistry. The concept of activation energy is significant in the world of science. Molecules require a certain threshold of energy to kickstart a chemical reaction. This is akin to the initial push you need to set your workday in motion. Just as molecules demand an energy infusion to overcome their barriers, you too can harness the power of physical activity to break through the barriers of fatigue, monotony and sluggishness.

As you go through your day, it's not uncommon to find yourself grappling with inertia, that unwelcome companion that threatens to hold you back. Imagine having a set of energising micro moves at your disposal – subtle yet powerful actions that can transform your static state into a dynamic state. A burst of physical activity, such as quickly standing up and sitting down again a few times, can provide the energy surge required to propel you into action. Though they take just a moment, the energising micro moves in your active workday toolkit can dismantle barriers and prepare you for focused, high-performance engagement.

Once the spark of activation energy ignites a chemical reaction, it typically sustains itself. Similarly, energising micro moves set off a chain reaction in your workday. As you engage in these brief bursts of activity, such as a power walk on the spot, you tap into an abundant source of momentum that propels your tasks and endeavours forward.

'I've realised that when I was sitting all day at work and not moving much, it was making me more tired. I got home and just wanted to crash on the couch and keep sitting! Now that

I've made a conscious effort to move more in my workday, I get home to my kids and I want to move with them. It's like a whole new level of energy and connection I didn't know was possible.' – Tim

Navigating the troughs with energising micro moves

You know those moments when you feel on top of the world, ready to conquer any task that comes your way – and then there are those times when you can barely keep your eyes open and you struggle to focus on the simplest tasks? Well, it turns out there's science behind these energy fluctuations, and understanding it can revolutionise how you approach your workday.

In his insightful book *When: The scientific secrets of perfect timing*, Daniel H. Pink delves into the hidden patterns of our daily lives, including the ebbs and flows of energy and cognitive abilities. He reveals that our productivity and wellbeing are not static but follow predictable daily patterns. It's like riding a wave, with peaks and troughs shaping our daily experience.

As the workday unfolds, it's inevitable that our energy hits a trough. Picture this as a gentle dip in our energy levels and cognitive performance, typically occurring during the early and mid-afternoon. It's the period when our eyelids become a bit heavier and our concentration starts to wane.

Here's the crucial part: ignoring the trough can lead us into dangerous territory. During the trough, our cognitive abilities take a hit. We're more prone to errors, our judgement becomes clouded and productivity slips through our fingers, as I mentioned at the start of this chapter. So, as much as we'd love to curl up for a power nap, most of us power on, often turning to caffeine or the tempting jar of biscuits to keep us going.

By strategically incorporating energising micro moves that work with your energy levels' natural ebbs and flows, you can gain a significant advantage in maximising your productivity, focus and overall wellbeing. So, whether it's a quick moment to get off your chair, do some squats or walk up and down a set of stairs, embrace the opportunity to incorporate energising micro moves into your daily routine. Follow this guide to counteract the challenges of the trough, boost your energy and unlock your full potential throughout the day.

Move to revitalise: make it through the mid-morning slump

You've been powering through your tasks and responsibilities for a couple of hours now and you may be starting to notice the effects of prolonged sitting and mental fatigue. Your body might feel a bit stiff or tense, and your concentration might be beginning to waver. Now is the right time to get up off your chair and get moving.

By embracing the mid-morning revitalisation, you proactively combat the mid-morning slump and infuse your workday with renewed vitality. This intentional boost sets the tone for increased productivity, improved focus and a positive mindset as you continue to navigate the day ahead.

So, give yourself permission to look away from your screen momentarily, stretch your legs and refresh your body. The move I'm going to show you now engages different muscle groups, improves circulation and increases your heart rate, giving you an instant burst of energy. When you return from your mid-morning refresh, you'll feel energised, focused and ready to tackle the tasks ahead.

TRY THIS: to scroll or to squat

Picture this. You're at work, feeling a bit drained and in need of a break. The dilemma arises: should you give in to the seductive allure of scrolling through your favourite social media feeds, or should you opt for something more physically engaging? Let's dive into the epic battle between the scrolling and the squatting breaks to determine which reigns supreme.

In the blue corner, we have the scrolling break. With just a few taps on your phone, you're transported into a digital wonderland filled with captivating posts and videos and endless scrolling. It's tempting, no doubt, but is it truly the refresher you need?

And in the red corner, we have the squatting break: taking a break from your seated position, standing up and engaging your leg and core muscles as you perform a series of squats. It requires a bit more effort, but does it deliver the energy boost you need?

Let's unveil the winner. Drumroll, please! Research shows that a break involving physical activity takes the crown as the better break for revitalising your energy levels. Why, you ask? Well, an exercise such as squats gets your blood flowing, increases your heart rate and engages multiple muscle groups, stimulating your body and mind in ways that scrolling just can't match.

By incorporating energising micro moves into your break routine, you activate your muscles, release tension and infuse yourself with a surge of revitalising energy. They're quick power-ups for both your body and your brain. On the other hand, the scrolling break, while entertaining and sometimes enticing, tends to keep us in a sedentary state. It may provide a temporary distraction, but it often leaves us feeling more mentally fatigued and less engaged when we return to our tasks.

So, the choice is yours: to scroll or to squat? It's clear that opting for an energising micro move not only invigorates your body but also enhances your mental clarity and focus. It's the ultimate break that fuels both your physical and cognitive wellbeing.

The next time you feel the urge to reach for your phone, consider taking a break for an energising micro move instead. Mix and match your moves to create your own customised break routine that suits your preferences and fitness level and gets your heart rate up. For example, you could go for ten squats and add a jump in between each if your body allows, challenge yourself with ten star jumps or try a 30 second jog on the spot as if the ground is hot (see chapter 6) – and if you really want to scroll through your socials, I guess you could do that at the same time.

Move to restore: maximising your lunch break

In our fast-paced work culture, it's easy to get caught up in the hustle and bustle of the day and overlook a simple yet powerful opportunity – the lunch break. Yes, that midday pause is when you can step away from your desk and nourish your body and mind.

One study revealed that the activities we choose to engage in during our lunch breaks can have a lasting impact on our energy levels. Participants who spent their lunch breaks taking part in activities that effectively helped them recover reported higher energy levels throughout the remainder of the workday. They felt less depleted and more energised by the end of the day.

Interestingly, certain specific activities had a more significant influence on sustained energy levels than others, and physical exercise and social interactions were found to be particularly beneficial for maintaining energy levels over time. Lunchtime is the perfect opportunity to reach into your active workday toolkit and do a micro move. Try the strength-boosting push-ups from chapter 8 or the mindset-boosting shadow boxing from chapter 9. Find a set of stairs and walk up and down a few times. Even better, find someone to move with you. In the study I mentioned just before, taking a walk during lunch breaks proved to be an effective strategy for boosting and preserving energy throughout the day – and it turns out there are plenty of reasons to move after lunch.

TRY THIS: balance blood sugar

After a fulfilling lunch, as the post-meal contentment washes over you, consider this simple yet powerful idea: instead of diving right back into your emails – assuming you even stepped away from your computer to eat – invest just two minutes in taking a walk. This isn't an insignificant stroll; it's a practice that researchers have discovered can potentially reshape your afternoon in unexpected ways.

Abrupt spikes and crashes in blood sugar levels can lead to serious health conditions, such as diabetes and heart disease. Here's where two-minute walks come into play. Roughly an hour after your meal, blood sugar levels tend to surge. Engaging in a brief walk after eating aligns perfectly with your body's natural processes. It assists your muscles in efficiently using the glucose from your meal, effectively transforming it into the fuel your body needs. By doing so, you actively help your body to maintain stable blood sugar levels and safeguard your long-term health.

According to the US Centers for Disease Control and Prevention, individuals who engage in around 150 minutes of physical activity each week have a 33 per cent reduced risk of all-cause mortality compared to those who are physically inactive. That 150 minutes a week translates to roughly 21 minutes of movement a day. You can break down those 21 minutes into ten two-minute micro walks throughout your day. Just a couple of minutes here and there, and you're achieving the recommended activity level, essentially lowering your risk of mortality from any cause by one-third. Considering the potential benefits, isn't that well worth the effort?

The magic of two-minute walks doesn't stop there. By preventing those notorious post-lunch energy dips caused by blood sugar crashes, these short walks provide you with a consistent and sustainable supply of energy throughout the afternoon. These steadier energy levels enable you to maintain productivity, alertness and engagement in your work, bridging the gap until you reach the well-known 3 p.m. slump – and stay tuned for the solution to that, too.

Moreover, two-minute walks positively influence your mood. Blood sugar fluctuations can lead to irritability and mood swings, particularly when levels drop rapidly. Engaging in these short walks and maintaining stable blood sugar levels can help you feel more positive and less stressed during your workday. This contributes to a better overall mood, making your work environment more enjoyable and your interactions with colleagues more pleasant.

Incorporating a mere two-minute walk after lunch – indoors or out – is a simple and achievable strategy to vitalise your energy, even with a busy schedule. After two minutes you might even keep going, but if not, remember that two minutes is better than no minutes!

Move to recharge: ride the wave

That mid-afternoon slump can be brutal. You've been powering through your work all day and suddenly you hit a wall. Your energy levels crash, your motivation wanes and the remaining hours of the day stretch out before you like an endless desert. To make matters worse, you still need to contemplate dinner plans, attend to family matters and tackle any lingering tasks on your to-do list.

So, what's the go-to solution for many of us when faced with this energy crisis? It often involves reaching for that fourth cup of coffee or into the biscuit jar. While these choices may provide a momentary energy boost, they come with their own set of downsides.

Coffee, with its caffeine content, can offer a temporary jolt of alertness, but this is often followed by an energy crash that leaves you feeling even more fatigued. Excessive caffeine intake can also disrupt your sleep patterns, making it difficult to get a good night's rest.

Sugary foods or beverages might provide a quick surge in energy, but this too is followed by a rapid crash. This rollercoaster effect can lead to increased hunger and irritability, not to mention the potential for weight gain and other health issues. Paradoxically, consuming excessive sugar can leave you feeling *more* tired – ironic, considering it's often our go-to energy boost.

The good news is that there's a healthier and more effective alternative to combat the mid-afternoon slump. When we feel tired and fatigued, our instinct may be to avoid physical activity, but research shows that incorporating short bursts of movement into our afternoons can combat that natural dip in energy. In fact, one research review found that the odds of feeling energetic were a whopping 60 per cent higher for those who embraced what they term 'micro-breaks' and 'energy management strategies' (described as 'a resource-replenishing strategy, taken informally between work tasks').

Another study found that 'microbouts' (as the researchers called them) of physical activity throughout the day decreased levels of fatigue and reduced food cravings more effectively than one longer 'bout' in the morning. Additionally, they found that taking regular breaks involving light physical activity, such as walking or stretching, can profoundly affect energy levels, mood, cognitive function and even food cravings.

Turning to your active workday toolkit for an energising micro move instead of resorting to excess caffeine or sugary options is a game-changer. By embracing the power of movement, you'll not only avoid the crash and burn of stimulants but also experience a sustainable and natural source of energy that keeps you going strong.

TRY THIS: sit-stand energy boost

You know when you've been glued to your chair for hours, staring at a screen, and suddenly your brain feels foggy? It's as if your mind is starved of the fuel it needs to function at its best. One effective technique to combat this cognitive decline and give you the boost you crave is to engage in an activity that will elevate your heart rate and activate your muscles, increase blood flow and oxygenation to the brain, and stimulate the release of neurotransmitters that enhance cognitive function. Let's add the sit-stand brain boost to your toolkit to do all this and more!

Start by rising from your chair. As you rise, focus on using your leg muscles to lift yourself off the chair, maintaining good posture and balance. You have the option here to reach your arms overhead, lengthen your spine and take a deep breath in. If you feel comfortable, you can lift both heels off the ground or even add a jump. Then, sit back down as you exhale. As you lower yourself back down, aim for a controlled descent, engaging your leg and core muscles. Aim to repeat the movement ten to 20 times. Go as fast or slow as feels good for you.

Looking for other energising options? Try doing a brisk ten to 20 'I've dropped my pen' reach-downs (see chapter 2), find a step and do some step-ups for 60 seconds, or put your hands on a sturdy desk or chair for some mountain-climber moves. You'll find videos and desk cards with demonstrations of these energising micro moves and more at lizziewilliamson.com/active.

Core points

- Despite the growing emphasis on self-care and wellbeing, a significant number of people find themselves grappling with low energy.
- The repercussions of energy depletion are far-reaching, affecting personal lives and careers, and even posing workplace hazards.
- When you partake in cardiovascular activities, your body releases endorphins – the body's natural energisers. This is the spark needed to reignite your energy.
- Think of the time of the day when you feel the least energised. This is the time to use a micro move as a 'spark' – do some squats or walk up and down the nearest staircase.
- The sit-stand recharging move is a brief yet impactful way to reset your focus and re-energise yourself. Aim stand up and sit down again ten times to break up long hours of sitting.

11

Elevate connection

Harnessing the power of movement for job satisfaction and joyful connections

The business of business is relationships;
the business of life is human connection.
Robin Sharma

In the age of messaging apps and virtual interactions, it's easier than ever to communicate. While these tools have undoubtedly improved efficiency and flexibility, they also come with a drawback: the potential for disconnection from our colleagues. Loneliness is creeping into our lives through the very devices meant to keep us connected.

Gone are the days of spontaneously popping by a colleague's desk for a quick chat or catching up over a coffee in the break room. Instead, we find ourselves typing out messages and sending emails, often missing out on the valuable face-to-face interactions that foster genuine connections. The nuances of body language, facial expressions and tone of voice, which play a significant role in understanding one another, are often lost.

The convenience of digital communication might save time, but it can also lead to a sense of isolation and disengagement within teams. While we may be interacting more frequently than ever through screens, the quality of these interactions can leave something to be desired. Loneliness in the workplace, once thought of as a personal issue, is now recognised as a significant problem making people less effective at work.

Loneliness and disconnection are complex and personal experiences that can affect individuals in various social settings, not just in remote work. Even in bustling offices surrounded by co-workers, people may feel disconnected and lonely for several reasons. These include a lack of meaningful connections in the workplace, workplace hierarchies or cultural differences that lead to feelings of alienation, transactional and work-focused communication, social anxiety, workplace cliques or exclusivity, mental health issues and personal life circumstances.

This is where movement can be a game-changer. By integrating movement into workplace interactions, you can create space for more genuine connections and bring back some of the energy and camaraderie that might be missing.

As we continue to adapt to the changing dynamics of the workplace, including the blend of physical and digital environments, it's crucial to find ways to bring back the human element and foster authentic connections. Movement provides a powerful tool to bridge this gap, fostering a sense of togetherness and joy that transcends the boundaries of physical distance or loneliness. Whether your workplace is traditional, remote or somewhere in between, movement can be the catalyst for enhanced job satisfaction and more meaningful connections among colleagues.

Embrace the awkwardness: movement in work interactions

There are often moments at work when connecting with others can feel intimidating or awkward. It's like attending a social event where you don't know anyone and find yourself hesitating to approach a group of strangers – you worry about being accepted or making the wrong impression. In the same way, introducing movement into your work interactions might initially seem like venturing into unfamiliar territory. You may wonder, *Will my colleagues think it's strange?* or *What if it disrupts the flow of the meeting?* These thoughts are part of a common resistance to trying something new even if it holds the potential for creating more meaningful connections and joy in the workplace.

Take a moment to remember the first time you tried riding a bicycle. It might have been nerve-wracking; you might have had wobbly balance and a fear of falling. But as you continued to practise and found your rhythm, the bicycle became a gateway to exploration and a sense of freedom. You were able to reach new places and experience the world in a whole different way.

Incorporating movement into your work interactions can be similar. Initially, you might feel uncertain and even a bit awkward. However, just like riding a bicycle, with practice and persistence, movement can become a powerful tool for building connections and cultivating a positive work environment.

For instance, you can start meetings with a quick ice-breaking movement exercise to set a positive and connected tone. Encourage everyone to stand up and perform a simple stretch, a few shoulder rolls or even a mini dance to a fun song. This small act can instantly lift spirits, break down barriers and make team members feel more engaged and present.

Imagine the camaraderie that comes from collectively participating in a fun movement exercise. Laughter and smiles abound as you all step out of your comfort zones together. It becomes a bonding moment, creating a sense of togetherness that can carry over into your work collaborations.

Movement meetings: the secret sauce for an active workplace

Megan was no stranger to the daily grind of back-to-back meetings. As she trudged from one meeting room to the next, it felt like a never-ending marathon. Some meetings were mercifully short, while others seemed to drag on indefinitely, testing her concentration to its limits. However, Megan had recently introduced a new secret weapon in her arsenal, a simple yet remarkably effective practice that had the power to breathe life into her meetings and turn them from mundane routines into engaging experiences: short bursts of movement with her colleagues at the start of each meeting.

'First and foremost,' Megan explained to me, 'you break out of the mundaneness of meeting after meeting, and it lifts your energy'.

Those short moments of movement at the start of her meetings were like shots of espresso for her mind. They helped her snap out of the repetitive daze that often accompanied the routine of meeting after meeting after meeting.

'Through the movement,' she continued, 'you have the chance to completely reset. You sit down afterwards and feel clear and energised. You become genuinely passionate about what's on the meeting agenda.'

For Megan, those brief moments of physical activity were like a reset button, pulling her out of the meeting fog and into a state of renewed focus.

'But there's more to it,' Megan grinned. 'You immediately connect with everyone in the meeting'.

It wasn't just about physical activity; it was also about breaking down barriers and forming genuine connections. The meeting moves had a way of drawing people in, breaking the ice and fostering real connections.

'I've done it with co-workers, even with external partners I'd never met before. They'd be in the meeting room and people outside could see us doing it. They were hesitant at first,' she admitted, 'but after the first movement, they got right into it. And you could see it on their faces – this is actually fun'.

It was evident that this unconventional approach had transformed Megan's meetings into more than just work discussions. They had become shared experiences, moments of genuine connection and levity. During those two minutes of movement, something shifted. It wasn't just about energy and connection; it was about enhanced cognitive abilities, sharper thinking and increased confidence.

'I think it makes you feel more on the ball, Megan added. 'You've got the clarity and you've got the energy,' she explained, 'but I feel like the ideas flow better. Your contributions are stronger. You feel confident just from that two-minute activity, and you're sitting down, connected, energised and ready to dive into the agenda. It makes meetings genuinely productive.'

A movement meeting is a unique approach designed to enhance connections between participants while infusing fun, smiles and laughter. It's all about injecting some joy and vitality into the workplace by introducing physical activity into otherwise sedentary meetings. These meetings provide accountability, reminders and a commitment to making both physical and mental wellbeing a top priority. They serve as a refreshing break from traditional meeting structures, encouraging participants to take a more active role in their own health and engagement.

You could start your meetings with some chairercise (chapter 2), a short walk on the spot (chapter 6) or posture power-ups (chapter 7) to get everyone moving and engaged. Alternatively, you might host stand-up meetings where people stand instead of sit around the conference table.

Movement isn't limited to the beginning of your meetings, either; it can also serve as a refreshing pause during longer meetings. Consider, for example, introducing a brain boosting micro breather (chapter 6) halfway through to re-energise the room and combat cognitive overload. At the end of an intense meeting, you might opt for a 'shake it off' moment (chapter 9), where everyone comes together for a quick and lively activity that not only rejuvenates spirits but also helps conclude the meeting on a positive note. You might take it all to the next level with a walking meeting (more on these in chapter 13), where you take discussions outdoors and enjoy fresh air and cognitive benefits as you walk and talk. All of these tactics aim to elevate connections, boost morale and create a lively atmosphere that enhances collaboration and productivity, all while letting you have a bit of fun along the way.

Movement meetings encourage active participation and engagement from all team members, regardless of location. As participants take a moment to move their bodies, they also move their minds, breaking free from mental rigidity and embracing a more open and receptive state. This energised collaboration leads to increased productivity and a sense of shared ownership in achieving team goals, whether in a physical meeting room or virtually.

TRY THIS: kickstart your meeting moves

Welcome to a new and innovative way of reimagining meetings and fostering a healthier, happier and more connected workplace. Meetings can sometimes become monotonous and the sedentary nature of these gatherings can take a toll on our physical and mental wellbeing, but we're about to fix that.

If introducing movement into your meetings feels daunting, don't worry. Here's a simple three-step plan to make this transition easy and enjoyable for everyone:

1. **Find a leader.** Look out for the fitness enthusiast or the person who loves to move in your team. Enlist them as your meeting movement champion. Having someone lead who is passionate about it can make the experience even more enjoyable for everyone. If you can't find a dedicated leader, no worries! Designate a different person each week to lead the group through an active micro move from this book. Don't worry, it doesn't have to be a professional dance routine – simple stretches and moves can work wonders.
2. **Find the moves.** At first you might encounter some resistance or hesitation from team members to lead or participate in the meeting moves. If that's the case, don't let it discourage you. Head over to my website, lizziewilliamson.com, where you'll find an array of engaging Two Minute Moves videos. Someone just has to press play and the meeting will instantly become a dynamic and uplifting experience. These videos will make it easy for anyone

to lead the team through energising movement exercises without any worry about coming up with routines.

3. **Explain the why.** At the start of your movement meetings, explain the reasons behind incorporating these active breaks into your gatherings. Let everyone know that there's more to these meeting moves than just having fun – although that's a big part of it! The science has your back: you're in for a healthier, happier and more connected workplace. When everyone understands the benefits of these meeting moves, they'll be more likely to embrace them wholeheartedly. So, don't be afraid to remind your team of the positive impact these simple and fun movements can have on their overall wellbeing and experience at work. Encourage everyone to participate at their own comfort level. Before you know it, any resistance people might have will soon turn to 'thank-you's.

Introducing the idea of meeting moves to your team can feel like a tricky task, but worry not: here are some scripts that can help you navigate this introduction, regardless of the specific micro moves you plan to incorporate. These conversational tools will help you to kickstart your next meeting and get your team enthusiastic about embracing these changes. Whether you're aiming to boost energy and focus, break free from sitting too long, stimulate creativity, foster team unity or relieve stress, there's a script to fit:

- 'Alright, team, let's kick off this meeting with some moves. Not only will they boost our energy and focus, but they also pump more oxygen to our brains and release those happy chemicals dopamine and serotonin. That means we'll feel more focused, alert and energised to tackle whatever comes our way. Ready? Let's go!'
- 'Time to beat the sitting slump. These meeting moves are our secret weapon. They help us break free from the clutches of too much sitting, keep our posture in check and keep our bodies

feeling flexible and happy. So, let's stretch those muscles and keep the energy flowing throughout the meeting.'

- 'Research shows that movement stimulates the memory and creativity centres in our brains, making us more imaginative and productive. We want to be creative and productive today, so let's dance our way to some amazing ideas and make this meeting truly inspiring.'
- 'Alright, team, time for some team-building magic. Taking a meeting move together is like a mini team-building adventure. It brings us all closer, strengthens our team bonds and makes us feel like we're part of one big family. So, let's create a happier team vibe with these moves.'
- 'Feeling the stress? Not for long! These meeting moves are like stress-relief superheroes. They unleash those endorphins – the natural mood lifters – and zap any tension or anxiety we might have. We'll leave the meeting with big smiles on our faces, feeling ready to conquer the world. Let's take this stress-busting journey together.'

Connection boost: elevating your workday with more fun

In your busy workday, have you ever stopped to ponder the lack of fun and excitement in your routine? The relentless stream of tasks and deadlines can leave little room for joy and spontaneity. It's a problem that many professionals face, and it can take its toll on your mood and wellbeing.

What if there was a simple yet effective way to infuse some fun and connection into your work life? Imagine a workday where, amid tasks and deadlines, there's a moment to hit the dance floor and let the music take you away. Dancing isn't just a fun way to break up the monotony of the day; it also comes with a plethora of health benefits that can transform your wellbeing and uplift your entire workplace.

Did you know that people over the age of 40 who participate in dancing almost halve their risk of dying from cardiovascular disease? It's true! Dancing is an incredible cardiovascular workout that gets your heart pumping and your blood flowing, contributing to a healthy heart and reduced risk of heart disease.

Beyond the physical benefits, dance has a profound impact on our mental and emotional health. As we dance with others, we smile, laugh and share in the collective enjoyment of the moment. The music and movement transport us to a place of happiness, making us forget about our stressors and worries. Dancing is a form of self-expression that allows us to connect with our body and emotions. It takes us to a space where we can let go of inhibitions, release tension and cultivate a positive outlook. Dance can be an outlet for creativity, a way to recharge your energy and an opportunity to connect with others on a deeper level.

Consider what my friend Amy has to say about dancing. Amy was the first person to read this book as I wrote it and, to my happiness, I started to infect her with my message. After reading this chapter she confessed this to me: 'Do you know what I do every lunchtime now? I put on the song 'Defying Gravity' from the musical *Wicked*, and I make up a dance routine in my living room – with gymnastics moves. It's what I used to do when I was a little girl and I realised it brings me exactly the same joy now. I look ridiculous, but I love it.'

Not only does it shake up her mood, but it also had an unexpected consequence – a bonding moment with her daughter. 'When my six-year-old got back from school one day, I showed her my routine and she told me I was cool – what a compliment,' laughed Amy. 'Now, most afternoons, we do two minutes of dance together. It transforms my mood, and it feels like we're creating core memories.'

In a work context, dancing might seem like an unconventional solution to boosting connection and having more fun. After all, work is often seen as a serious and focused endeavour. However, in my experience of helping people incorporate dancing into their workdays and meetings, it can have a remarkable impact on team dynamics and individual wellbeing. It breaks down barriers, fosters creativity and brings an element of joy that can transform connections, both at work and beyond. Dancing adds an unexpected but delightful dimension to the workday, and it's a powerful tool for building stronger, more positive relationships among colleagues.

Try this: take a dance break

So, why not bring dance into your workday through dance breaks? Whether in the office or online, organising a quick dance session can inject a burst of enthusiasm and positive energy into the work environment. Dance breaks are perfect for combatting the 3 p.m. slump and waning energy levels. One fantastic song (suggestions in just a moment) can be just what you need to recharge and refocus for the rest of the day.

From small start-ups to multinational corporations, I've seen dance breaks work wonders in transforming workplace dynamics. They promote a healthy and joyful work environment, encourage teamwork and create lasting memories. The best part is, you don't need to be a professional dancer to enjoy the benefits – everyone can join in and there's no judgement on the dance floor.

So, it's time to pump up the volume and let that perfect song light up your soul! Get your colleagues together, kick off your shoes (metaphorically or literally) and dance like there's no tomorrow. Who cares whether or not your moves are funky or fresh? The goal is to have a blast, bond with your team and create an unforgettable sense of connection.

To make dance breaks even more engaging, consider offering prizes for the most enthusiastic dancer or the most creative moves. This friendly competition can further encourage participation and infuse even more fun into the dance sessions. (More on the benefits of competition to come in chapter 16.)

As a professional speaker, bringing the energy to company meetings, offsites, events and conferences is what I do best. I have tried-and-tested dance routines that never fail to get people up on their feet, grooving and having a blast. Whether it's a team-building event, a corporate conference or a casual offsite, these three iconic songs and respective, almost universally known dance moves inject an instant burst of enthusiasm and camaraderie into any setting:

1. When I lead **'Y.M.C.A.' by The Village People**, I see teams forming those iconic letters with their arms, bonding over shared laughter and building a sense of unity. It's incredible how quickly the energy in the room shifts and participants become fully immersed in the moment.
2. **'Macarena' by Los Del Rio** transcends age and background. From top executives to new hires, everyone joins in on the fun, following the simple steps and feeling the rhythm together. This song is all about contagious joy and carefree dancing.
3. Lastly, **'Nutbush City Limits' by Tina Turner** adds a nostalgic touch, reminding attendees of cherished memories and carefree times. As they dance in unison, the room transforms into a vibrant celebration of teamwork and shared experiences.

Pop these songs on and witness firsthand the transformation in the room – from reserved individuals to a united and exuberant group. Everyone is usually very surprised just how much people commit to the moves! It's an incredible thing to experience.

Your workplace dance playlist

Research suggests uplifting music is like a 'performance-enhancing drug', so hit the floor and feel the rhythm with these dance anthems:

- 'Dancing Queen', ABBA
- 'I Wanna Dance with Somebody (Who Loves Me)', Whitney Houston
- 'You Should Be Dancing', Bee Gees
- 'Dance Monkey', Tones and I
- 'Just Dance', Lady Gaga ft. Colby O'Donis.

Head to lizziewilliamson.com/active for my mood-boosting playlist.

Core points

- Loneliness in the workplace is now recognised as a significant problem. This is where movement can be a game-changer.
- Incorporating movement into your work interactions can feel awkward at first, but it does get easier – especially when you begin to reap the collective benefits.
- Start meetings, whether online or in person, with quick ice-breaking movements to set a positive and connected tone. It creates a bond, even if it's just a shared awkwardness initially!
- Consider swapping your sit-down meetings for standing meetings or incorporate movement into the beginning of your team brainstorming session.
- Remember, any new habit feels strange at first. My advice is this: don't take it too seriously. This is a great way to incorporate more joy and play into your workday.

Part III
Revolutionise
The active workday framework

Welcome to the part of *The Active Workday Advantage* that heralds a powerful transformation within your organisation. This is where you'll find your opportunity to extend your active workday beyond yourself and your individual practices – to embrace change, champion wellbeing and ignite a revolution in the organisations and communities you work within.

In the first two parts of this book, you reimagined and redesigned your workday. You embarked on a journey to unlock your most energised, engaged and happy self at work. You recognised the importance of understanding your motivations, overcame obstacles, charted a course and reinforced positive habits. Now it's time to take that transformation to the next level. It's time to bring these principles to life in your workplace and create an active, dynamic environment that benefits not only you but also everyone you work with.

The active workday is a revolution, and it's not just about physical activity; it's about fostering a culture that values wellbeing, vitality and collective achievement. It's about starting a movement inside your organisation to challenge the status quo and propel everyone towards a shared goal.

This section is vital for leaders and managers, but it's also important for individual team members. We can all model the active workday, and we can all play a part in creating a culture where prioritising physical and mental health in the workday is the norm – and, as you'll discover, when a culture changes, everyone benefits.

Introducing the framework for an active revolution

So, you're keen to join the revolution and help your organisation to become an active workplace. You're eager for everyone around you to experience the active workday advantage. Hooray! But where do you start, and how do you make this vision a reality? The answer lies in the active workday framework.

The active workday framework is a comprehensive plan to make your workplace more active and engaging, a vibrant place of wellbeing and productivity. It's a carefully planned route that supports the stability, reputation and overall success of your business by bolstering the health and happiness of its employees; it's win-win scenario for both organisations and people.

The process of creating an active workplace comprises five key phases, each laying a robust foundation for the next. In the five chapters that follow, we'll dive into each of these phases, unravelling the questions they pose and the actions they demand.

The first phase is conducting research that will arm you with insights and data essential for igniting the active revolution in your workplace. This will be the compass that steers you towards both opportunities and areas in need of improvement.

The second phase of the active workday framework is leading by example. This is where you'll learn to become your own active role model and inspire your colleagues – whether you're a member of the leadership team or not.

Defining your destination is the pivotal next phase of the active workday framework. At this critical point, you'll sculpt a vivid vision and mission statement, establish clear, actionable objectives and craft an inspiring manifesto that will serve as your compass, guiding you and your organisation towards a future where an active workday is not merely a routine but also a vibrant way of life.

The next phase, in which you design your roadmap, marks a strategic turn in the active workday framework. This is where the abstract vision and mission statements are translated into tangible action plans. Your roadmap takes those lofty aspirations and breaks them down into manageable, actionable goals and objectives. It's the bridge between dreams and reality, charting a clear path to transform your workplace into a dynamic, active environment that benefits everyone.

In the final phase of the active workday framework, it's time to rally your people and transform bystanders into active participants – into champions. By cultivating a sense of collective responsibility, you'll be able to work together to bring your vibrant workplace vision to life.

With this framework in hand, get ready to champion change, spearhead a movement and be part of the active revolution at your workplace. Your journey starts here.

12

Do your research

Igniting a revolution

You never change things by fighting the existing reality.
To change something, build a new model that makes the existing model obsolete.

Buckminster Fuller

The pages of history are marked by revolutions that have transformed societies, economies and cultures. One of the most significant revolutions that reshaped the world was the industrial revolution – a period of rapid change characterised by technological advancements, urbanisation and shifts in labour practices. As industries boomed and economies grew, a new era emerged, shaping the modern work landscape. The industrial revolution brought about unprecedented progress and innovation, but it also laid the groundwork for some of the work-related challenges we face today. Long working hours, sedentary jobs and a disconnect between physical wellbeing and productivity became ingrained in work culture.

Physical activity in the workplace has significantly declined over the last five decades, primarily due to the widespread adoption of computers and digital technology. This shift has resulted in prolonged periods of sitting, especially in office and administrative jobs. In Australia, more than 11 million people spend an average of eight hours a day at their workplaces. Shockingly, over two-thirds of the typical office workday involves being sedentary, with much of this time being spent in uninterrupted periods of 30 minutes or more. This extended sitting has been shown to have negative consequences for our physical and mental health.

It's becoming widely acknowledged, both nationally and internationally, that the workplace is a crucial and influential setting for implementing interventions to promote healthier behaviours. Governments worldwide have incorporated explicit messages into their physical activity and sedentary behaviour guidelines emphasising the urgency to minimise prolonged sitting and interrupt extended periods of inactivity whenever possible. Unfortunately, we're falling short of meeting these guidelines. Nearly six in ten Australian adults (and over eight in ten children and young people) do not meet recommended activity levels. This places Australia among the countries with the lowest levels of physical activity in the world.

What's next? The active workday revolution

The industrial revolution changed work the world over, and the active workday revolution seeks to once again reshape how we approach work and productivity, with an additional focus on wellbeing. It's a response to the growing realisation of governments, organisations and individuals that regularly breaking up long hours of sitting in our work lives is intimately tied to our overall health and vitality.

The shift towards an active workday answers the changing needs and expectations of the modern workforce. The days of equating productivity with prolonged hours of sedentary work are giving way to an understanding that movement, physical activity and wellbeing are integral to optimal performance. The active workday revolution recognises that a healthier, more active workforce is not only more engaged and productive but also happier and better equipped to face the challenges of the modern workplace.

It's not about just adding a free yoga class or providing ergonomic chairs. It's about a fundamental shift in mindset and culture –

a transformation that places wellbeing at the forefront of work practices. It's about empowering individuals to take control of their health, encouraging organisations to foster environments that support movement and recognising that a thriving workforce is an asset to both employees and employers.

Picture your workplace as an energetic hub where everyone enjoys the benefits of regular movement. Imagine a vibrant atmosphere that supports people to break up sitting time with their active workday toolkit and revitalise their minds and bodies. Creating an active workplace isn't a passing trend; it's an essential transformation. The time for action is now, and it's essential for the wellbeing and productivity of your workforce.

Workplaces that actively support and prioritise an active workday radiate energy distinct from traditional work environments. It's palpable, from the moment you walk into the office – the open stances, smiles and connection between the people working there are unmistakable. Even in remote settings you can sense it during meetings from participants' manners and relaxed expressions. Transitioning from a sedentary workday to an active workday can transform an exhausted and disengaged workforce into an energised, motivated and happy group of people with a common goal. The positive impact on employee experience, satisfaction and performance is undeniable.

For readers with financial accounting or CFO backgrounds – and those seeking buy-in from management – the financial implications of prioritising employee wellbeing are important. As you know, neglecting to invest in your workforce can lead to various financial challenges. When it comes to health and wellness, this can manifest as increased stress leave, sick leave and higher employee turnover, all of which have a significant impact on your bottom line. By investing in your people's wellness upfront, whether by allocating additional resources, implementing specific programs or simply encouraging physical activity, you're actively mitigating the financial risks associated with employee illness, high turnover and reduced performance. Physical activity plays a crucial role as it directly contributes to improved health and reduced stress levels among employees.

It all comes down to the idea that happy and healthy employees lead to satisfied customers, which ultimately drives profits. Your people should be considered your organisation's number-one asset. When you prioritise their wellbeing and create a supportive work environment that includes opportunities and support for physical activity, the profits are likely to follow. Essentially, the active workday advantage isn't just about fostering a positive workplace culture; it's also about recognising the positive impact that physical activity can have on the overall health and performance of your team and how this, in turn, can contribute to your business's long-term success and financial stability.

Why an active workplace matters for company culture

Physical activity is a powerful force that can invigorate every corner of your organisation and energise the very core of your workplace dynamics. Having read the first two parts of this book, you'll have a fair idea of the benefits that await, but here are three key reasons why integrating movement into company culture – not just individually – is both vital and transformative.

The first concerns wellbeing and productivity. Researchers have found that happy employees are approximately 12 per cent more productive than their less happy counterparts and note companies that prioritise employee support and satisfaction have experienced significant improvements in productivity as a result. According to these researchers, the key factor behind this productivity boost is that happier employees use their time more effectively, allowing them to work at a faster pace without compromising quality. Another study discovered that employees who engage in workplace exercise programs experience a remarkable 72 per cent enhancement in their time management and workload completion. The ripple effect from these programs is greater focus, creativity and overall performance – what's not to like?

A culture of movement also fosters a sense of camaraderie and connection among your team members. Shared moments of stretching, walking meetings and collective movement breaks create opportunities for employees to engage with one another beyond the confines of tasks and deadlines. As a result, bonds strengthen, collaboration deepens and a positive sense of community flourishes. When movement becomes part of your organisation's identity, it shapes interactions and relationships, leading to a more vibrant and connected workplace. Remember, too, the body's very own chill pills. Essentially, movement triggers an increased release of endocannabinoids, naturally occurring compounds in the body, resulting in a heightened sense of enjoyment during social engagements and a reduction in barriers that might hinder connections.

Finally, in today's competitive job market, attracting and retaining top talent is crucial for the success of any organisation. A company that can proudly proclaim 'We are an active workplace' becomes highly attractive to potential employees. Job seekers are increasingly drawn to workplaces that offer a holistic approach to employee care, and a culture of movement signals that your company values its employees' health, happiness and wellbeing. It not only sets you apart from other employers but also acts as a magnet for individuals who seek a vibrant and engaging work environment.

In short, incorporating movement into your company culture becomes a compelling selling point when recruiting new talent. It showcases your commitment to creating a workplace that promotes both professional growth and personal wellbeing. This means that you not only enhance your current team's performance but also ensure a steady influx of top-tier talent eager to contribute to your company's success.

A return on investment: active employees

Beyond the less tangible benefits, integrating movement into company culture can yield substantial financial gains. Healthier employees are less prone to illness and absenteeism, contributing to reduced healthcare costs. Moreover, a vibrant and active workforce is linked to increased productivity and decreased turnover rates, ultimately translating into significant financial savings for your organisation.

As I've mentioned, research indicates that incorporating exercise breaks into the workday can significantly enhance performance. By investing in movement, you're not just promoting wellbeing; you're also making smart business decisions with measurable returns. One report showed that every dollar directed towards workplace wellness initiatives, such as exercise, yields a substantial return of $2.30. Research has also found that companies with more than four engaged employees for every employee who was disengaged experienced 2.6 times greater growth in earnings compared to companies in their industry with a lower ratio of engaged workers. In simpler terms, businesses with more motivated and committed employees outperformed their competitors in terms of financial growth.

Promoting physical activity in the workplace for health reasons isn't merely another checkbox on the wellness agenda – it's also smart for businesses and the economy. Inactivity is having a huge impact globally, and if we don't address it, it will only get worse, costing a mind-boggling US$300 billion in the decade leading up to 2030 with 500 million new cases of preventable diseases!

'Absenteeism' refers to time away from work due to illness. Meanwhile 'presenteeism' describes employees being physically present at work but, due to various factors such as illness, personal circumstances, exhaustion and burnout, being unable to be productive or perform well, which manifests as reduced productivity. Together, absenteeism and presenteeism create a big problem for businesses of all sizes and in all industries. A recent report prepared for Pathology Awareness Australia has quantified the cost of presenteeism in the Australian economy at a substantial $34 billion per annum. But the impact goes beyond just money – it affects the whole vibe of the workplace. If physical inactivity isn't taken seriously, it can lead to higher staff turnover, lower employee happiness and more burnout and stress-related issues among the team. Encouraging employees to get moving isn't just good for the bottom line; it's about creating a workplace where everyone can thrive.

The good news is that studies show that promoting physical activity among employee populations can help prevent and reduce absenteeism and presenteeism. Employers can tackle these challenges head-on and make a positive difference. By providing support and resources, businesses can save money in the long run. It's a win-win!

So, let's work together to turn the idea of an active workday into a vibrant reality. We've already established the 'why', and now it's time to transition into the 'how'. The journey commences with a deep understanding of your current workplace dynamics. Once you know your starting point, you can chart the course to where you want to be: a workplace brimming with energy and activity. Together, we'll make it happen.

How to begin: laying the foundations

The revolution for an active workday requires a vibrant movement within your organisation. With your unique vantage point, plugged into the dynamics of your work, your business and your team, you are poised to generate and guide this transformation. Your passion for a healthier, more active workday makes you the perfect person to drive this revolution and instigate positive change within your workplace.

As you embark on this journey, the first crucial step is a thorough examination of your workplace at present. This will give you valuable insights with which to begin creating change. Just as you wouldn't want a new employee with no idea about what the business is doing or its history to waltz in on their first day and tell everyone what to do, you don't want to start trying to transform your workplace without laying a solid foundation.

This research-driven foundation serves as the first proof point that will guide you towards turning the lofty idea of an active workplace into a practical reality. Here is a plan to do your research – the first phase in the active workday framework.

Step 1: survey the team

In the initial stages of research, understanding the nuances of your workday – and your colleagues' workdays – is crucial. Surveys are an effective way to gather insights and can feature simple-to-answer multiple-choice and open-ended questions. They will guide your journey towards creating a more active workplace by providing a platform for every voice to be heard and contributing to a comprehensive understanding of your workplace's current landscape.

Here are some sample questions to draw from as you construct a survey relevant to your people:

- On average, how many hours do you spend sitting at work?
- How often do you take breaks from sitting in the same position?
- What types of physical activity would you be interested in incorporating into your workday?
- On a scale of one to ten, with one being not motivated at all and ten being highly motivated, how motivated are you to make your workday more active?

Questions like these invite employees to share their daily routines, challenges and aspirations. (Download a full set of sample questions at lizziewilliamson.com/active.) The answers can paint a comprehensive picture of your workplace's activity.

Step 2: talk to your people

Though surveys offer valuable insights, they only reveal part of the picture. To gain a deeper understanding of your work environment, it's essential to also engage in meaningful conversations. These interviews go beyond data collection; they are windows into the experiences, challenges and aspirations of employees of various departments and seniority. They are candid discussions that provide a holistic view of the daily dynamics that shape your workplace culture. By hearing from employees across different roles, you can identify potential bottlenecks and challenges.

If you're a manager, consider enlisting the support of 'movement champions' (discussed in chapter 13) to connect with team members. Their insights can provide a deeper understanding of what's happening at a grassroots level. Here are some sample interview questions:

- How does your workday affect your wellbeing and productivity?
- Can you share examples of moments when you've struggled with being active during your workday?
- Do you feel encouraged or permitted to get up and move around during your workday?
- What, in your opinion, is the most significant roadblock preventing you from being more physically active during your workday?

These interviews, filled with personal anecdotes and unique perspectives, will provide profound insights that complement the survey data, offering a more nuanced understanding of what's happening on the ground.

These insights are especially significant because they provide a glimpse into the lived experience within your organisation, which may differ from the corporate culture and marketing messages. While surveys provide a temperature check, these conversations and insights are a reality check, ensuring a comprehensive view of your organisation's current state.

Step 3: draw from personal experience

Your personal workplace experiences are incredibly valuable. As you gather survey responses and engage in conversations, your unique insights should contribute a personal dimension to the research.

Incorporate personal anecdotes into the ongoing dialogue, ensuring that the research process is both relatable and responsive to the diverse perspectives within your organisation.

Core points

- The workplace is an influential setting for promoting healthier behaviours.
- A vibrant and active workforce is linked to increased productivity and decreased turnover rates, ultimately translating into financial savings for your organisation.
- It's not about just adding a free yoga class or providing ergonomic chairs. It's about a fundamental shift in mindset and culture.
- The magnetic capacity of movement can rally people behind a common cause – a different way of approaching work that prioritises wellbeing, energy and a more dynamic workplace.
- Talk to your people – surveys and meaningful conversations with employees of all roles will help identify the state of play and navigate the path to a more active workplace.

13

Be a role model

Leading with social influence

If not me, then who? If not now, then when?

Emma Watson

In the intricate tapestry of human behaviour, a potent thread runs through our decisions and actions: the influence of our peers. This phenomenon, known as 'social influence', underscores our innate inclination to align ourselves with the actions and choices of those around us. In the workplace, harnessing the dynamics of social influence can transform a sedentary routine into an active workday.

The influence that individuals can have on their peers is often underestimated. This influence, driven by colleagues inspiring and motivating each other, has the potential to bring about significant positive change within an organisation. It's a valuable force that should be recognised and leveraged.

Time and again I've had the privilege of observing this phenomenon of social influence in action, igniting the spirits of individuals from diverse fields – be they accountants or architects, bankers or business owners, engineers or educators, CEOs or software developers, lawyers or librarians, miners or managers, tech support or teachers, nurses, veterinarians... the list goes on. When I present to these groups, the event organiser often feels a hint of uncertainty to begin with, fearing that nobody will join in. However, without fail, momentum builds and everyone ends up engaging.

> *'We had Lizzie to help with our focus on wellbeing and to keep our people energised throughout the day. I wasn't sure how everyone would react, but they were up and moving in no time.' – Emma*

Have you ever noticed how a single person's actions can inspire others to follow suit? It's similar to when one person starts dancing at a party and suddenly the entire room joins in. The same principle applies when colleagues embrace an active workday – they convey the message that taking care of oneself is not just acceptable but encouraged.

Imagine this scenario. A colleague suggests a walking meeting instead of a conventional sit-down discussion. While seemingly minor, this choice is influential. Others witness it and think, *If they can do it, so can I.* That individual's decision ignites a spark and grants everyone else permission to break from the norm and prioritise their wellbeing.

Both leaders and team members can use social influence as a tool for bringing physical activity into their workplaces. When teammates integrate movement into their daily routine and leaders encourage and support it, they set a new, active tone. They alter workplace dynamics forever – and for the better. Suddenly, movement isn't an outlier; it's an integral part of our shared journey. As more of us take that step, it evolves into the standard. This is the essence of social influence – it transforms a personal choice into a collective practice, lighting the path towards an active and vibrant work environment.

Champion an active workday advantage: absolutely everybody can do it

Leading by example is a potent way to initiate the active workday movement. It's crucial to recognise that leadership and influence aren't confined to executives or managers; every individual within an organisation has the potential to inspire change through their actions.

Irrespective of your position or role, you have the power to set an example by seamlessly integrating movement into your daily work routine. You can do this by starting your meetings with a quick, energising exercise, going for walking meetings or encouraging your colleagues to participate in micro moves with you. These actions not only demonstrate your commitment to the cause but also encourage others to join in and make the active workday a shared reality.

Remember that your actions can resonate profoundly with your colleagues. When they see you actively embracing a healthier work routine, they're more likely to follow suit. By becoming a champion for an active workday, you can lead the charge towards a healthier, more vibrant workplace for everyone. Your role as a leader, in this case, is not defined by your title but by your actions and the inspiration you provide to your team.

Top down: giving the green light to your team

Almost every time I lead a workshop and ask what everyone needs in order to embrace an active workday, someone raises their hand and says, 'We need our leaders to not just *say* it's okay, but to actually *do it themselves*'. People seem to want a green light to take those much-needed active breaks and make movement a priority. Guess who they're looking to for this assurance: the people who conduct their performance reviews and shape their work environment.

I've heard this sentiment time and again from employees. They want to know that it's not only acceptable but actively encouraged to infuse movement into their workday. They're seeking a cue, a signal that it's alright to stretch their legs, take a breather and do something for their wellbeing. That cue often comes from the actions of those they look up to – their leaders, managers and CEOs.

Leadership is more than just a title – it's a commitment to guide, inspire and create positive change. As Simon Sinek famously wrote, 'Leadership is not about being in charge. Leadership is about taking care of those in your charge'. When leaders step up and demonstrate the value of movement, it sends a powerful message. It says, 'We're all in this together – and your wellbeing matters'. This leadership style erases the invisible line between hierarchy and teamwork, turning the workplace into a place of shared commitment. It encourages employees to shatter the chains of inactivity, knowing that they're not alone in their quest for movement.

In a recent virtual workshop I did with a global software company, the CEO walked the walk – literally. She joined the session with her camera on and showed everyone how it's done. Her genuine participation set an example and created a comfortable space for everyone to follow suit. With her leading from the front, the team felt accountable and encouraged to turn on their cameras, embrace the movements and even share a few laughs about the CEO's dance moves.

As we covered in chapter 11, this moment wasn't just about getting some physical activity in; it was also about connection, trust and camaraderie. This type of leadership paves the way for a cultural shift in the workplace that embraces movement, prioritises wellbeing and fosters a sense of unity within the organisation.

TRY THIS: experiment with your toolkit

You can model an active approach to your workday by inviting your colleagues to join you as you experiment with your active workday toolkit. One way to begin is by starting your meetings with a brief energising exercise or stretching routine to set a positive tone and encourage others to follow suit. Another idea is taking a walk while on the phone with a colleague – and don't forget to explain why. You might, for example, mention that you're embracing the benefits of walking meetings, including enhanced creativity and reduced sedentary time, and encourage your colleague to join you. Additionally, you can demonstrate leadership by consistently sharing success stories and outcomes related to the active workday initiative, showcasing how it positively impacts on your work and wellbeing. This encourages your team to follow your lead and actively participate in the movement towards an active workday.

As you craft a movement-infused culture within your organisation, remember that often the most effective cues come from the top. This means that if you're in a leadership position, what you say and do matters. Additionally, by authentically embodying the practice, you provide more than permission – you provide inspiration.

I've put together a selection of inspiring ideas to share with your leadership team in a document downloadable from lizziewilliamson.com/active. This resource will assist them in setting an example for an active workday, encouraging others to follow suit.

Bottom up: actions speak louder than words

Whether you're on the leadership team or not, you can spark a movement that transforms the way your colleagues approach their work and wellbeing by simply leading by example. You can have your very own active workday and still be a key player in creating a healthier, more vibrant active workplace.

Remember, actions speak louder than words. When colleagues see your dedication to an active workday, they'll be inspired and empowered to make positive changes themselves. I'll give you more targeted support in the next chapter, but here are five impactful ways you can revolutionise your workday and inspire others to do the same:

- Incorporate active rituals, such as opening meetings with some micro moves.
- Prioritise breaking up your workday with movement.
- Host walking meetings.
- Share your success.
- Engage in team challenges.

The first step is practising what you preach by integrating movement into your daily routine. Dip into your active workday toolbox by starting your day with a morning stretch and bookending it with a quick session of chair yoga (see chapter 9), for example. When your colleagues see your commitment to movement, the gears will begin to turn.

Set an example by taking regular moments of movement throughout the day. Stand up, stretch and encourage your colleagues to join you in a brief walk around the office. As you know, these breaks not only rejuvenate the body but also foster a culture of active engagement. The next level is swapping traditional conference-room meetings for walking meetings. Lead discussions while strolling through the office or outdoors. Your proactive approach will show that movement doesn't have to be a separate activity – it can seamlessly integrate into your work routine.

Remember, the goal is to make your active workday achievable, consistent and tailored to your needs. There is no one-size-fits-all approach. However, if you believe that having something to follow would be beneficial, you can explore a variety of active workday guides at lizziewilliamson.com/active. There you'll find guides suited for different work environments, whether you're working from home or in an open-plan office.

Don't be shy about sharing your success and be sure to communicate the positive impact of an active workday on your own wellbeing. Whether it's improved focus, increased energy or reduced stress, sharing your experiences will make the concept relatable and compelling for your colleagues. Finally, participate wholeheartedly in wellness challenges and encourage your colleagues to join you. By showcasing your commitment and enthusiasm, you create an atmosphere of camaraderie that motivates everyone to contribute to an active workplace.

TRY THIS: step outside with walking meetings

Walking meetings are not your traditional sit-down gatherings; they are dynamic, refreshing and, as many have found, transformational. These meetings involve taking your discussions and brainstorming sessions outdoors or around your workspace while walking and talking. The concept might sound simple, but its effects on creativity, productivity and overall wellbeing are profound.

When you step out into the open air, stroll through the office or even pace around your space while discussing business matters on the phone, you're not just moving your body; you're also freeing your mind. Research has shown that physical activity, even in the form of a leisurely walk, can stimulate creative thinking and boost problem-solving abilities. So, why not try walking meetings and see if they help your team to think differently, encourage outside-the-box solutions and engage in more productive conversations?

In addition to enhancing creativity, walking meetings promote collaboration. The act of walking side by side rather than facing each other across a table creates a less formal and more equal footing, often leading to more open, honest and fruitful discussions. It removes hierarchical barriers and fosters a sense of unity and teamwork. When you take your meetings outdoors or through your workplace, whether in person or on the phone, you enable social interaction that enhances relationships and strengthens your work culture.

Can you have walking meetings virtually? Absolutely! Using a reliable video conferencing app you can bring the same dynamic experience of an in-person walking meeting to a virtual setting – or you could simply make it a phone call. As you walk and talk, the conversation becomes more engaging, fostering a sense of connectedness and camaraderie, even when participants are miles apart. Can't leave your desk? Stand up and walk around your home or office. It's incredible how much of a positive impact a simple walk can have on a conversation.

Whether in-person or virtual, walking meetings offer a refreshing departure from the norm, making them a valuable tool for any organisation looking to inject new life into their work discussions and promote wellbeing among their team.

A simple school initiative: the Daily Mile

The Daily Mile is an initiative that started in 2012 with a single school in Scotland and has since become a global phenomenon transforming the lives of young learners. The brilliance lies in its simplicity: children run, jog or walk together for just 15 minutes each day – and the results have been astonishing.

The Daily Mile not only improves physical fitness but also boosts mental wellbeing, concentration and social interaction among students. Reports reveal that participating children experience increased levels of happiness and self-esteem. What began as a humble endeavour to address the lack of physical activity in children has become a movement endorsed by governments, educators and health professionals worldwide.

The very principles that make the Daily Mile a school superstar can also apply to our professional playground. The simplicity of the idea, the incorporation of regular movement and the positive impact on overall wellbeing are all elements that resonate within the professional context. Imagine taking a brief break each day to step away from desks, walk or jog together and reconnect with colleagues in a refreshing way. Beyond enhancing physical health, this practice could foster a sense of unity, invigorate minds and create a shared experience that strengthens our bonds with one another.

Being brave: break the stigma of movement

In many workplaces there's an underlying stigma associated with getting up and moving around during the workday. It's as if taking a moment to stretch or do a quick exercise is a sign of slacking off or lacking dedication to the job. As you know, this mentality comes at a price – and the idea it represents couldn't be further from the truth. Incorporating movement into your workday is *not* a sign of laziness; rather, it's a sign of self-care and a commitment to your wellbeing. It's a conscious choice to prioritise your health so that you can be more productive, focused and engaged in your work.

It can be challenging to be the first to break the mould, to stand up and stretch or to do a quick micro move when everyone else is glued to their desks. There can be a fear of judgement and a worry that colleagues or superiors might perceive you differently. It's the elephant in the room – the unspoken barrier that keeps us in our chairs. Don't let this hold you back. Instead, consider this book permission to take initiative, incorporate movement into your workday and set a positive example for your colleagues. You can inspire others to prioritise their health and wellbeing by living your values and inviting your colleagues to join you.

As I mentioned at the start of this book, the active workday starts with a shift in perspective. Instead of viewing movement as a distraction from work, see it as an enhancement of your work. Movement isn't the enemy of productivity; it's its ally. By investing in your physical health, you're investing in your ability to excel at your job.

Let's break the stigma together. Let's create a workplace culture where movement is not only accepted but encouraged. Let's make it the new norm to prioritise our wellbeing and incorporate micro moves into our workdays without fear of judgement. In doing so, we'll not only transform our own work experience but also inspire a healthier, happier and more productive work environment for all. We'll become movement champions.

Becoming a movement champion

> *'I have introduced some of your active ideas into my workplace. I was worried my colleagues would think I was mad, but it has been awesome. People keep asking me for more!' – Joseph*

The active workday revolution is calling for champions to step up, energise and lead the way to a healthier and more vibrant work environment. Movement champions are catalysts for cultural transformation within an organisation. As beacons of inspiration and agents of change, they lead the charge in fostering a workplace environment that values movement, wellbeing and holistic health. By embodying the principles of an active workday, movement champions showcase how small, deliberate actions can collectively create a positive shift in company culture. Their dedication not only elevates individual wellbeing but also serves as a driving force for increased engagement, collaboration and productivity among colleagues.

> *'When you hear about wellbeing from a colleague, from someone you trust, that person you can sit down with for a friendly chat or share a cup of tea with – a person already embedded in your team – it carries a different weight.' – Bec*

As role models and social influencers, movement champions are the heart and soul of a workplace transformation, igniting a movement that binds the workforce in the pursuit of a healthier, more invigorating professional journey. Embracing the role of movement champion offers the chance to not only inspire others through example but also to become the cartographer of a roadmap leading to a dynamic, active workforce. It's an opportunity to be at the forefront of a thriving, vibrant workplace revolution.

Introducing something new into your workplace might seem daunting, but rest assured it's a valuable investment. By taking the lead in fostering an active workday, you'll be at the forefront of energising, engaging and bringing happiness to your workforce. If you're concerned that your colleagues might resist the movement you're building, keep in mind the experience of countless individuals I've worked with: though there might initially be some groans at the thought of getting active, those often turn into a chorus of 'thank-you's. Get ready for an abundance of gratitude from the people you work with.

Speaking of personal benefits, being a movement champion who helps create and share this roadmap also elevates your profile within your workplace. It's an excellent way to impress your boss and enhance your CV, demonstrating both your commitment to cultivating a healthier workplace culture and your leadership skills. Your dedication to driving positive change speaks volumes about your priorities, benefiting not only your wellbeing but also the wellbeing of your colleagues.

If you're ready to lead the revolution, here's an email template you could send to your leaders to kickstart the movement:

> **Subject: Forming a team of movement champions – sparking a healthier workplace**
>
> Dear [name],
>
> I wanted to share an idea that I believe holds great potential for enhancing our workplace culture and employee wellbeing. As we continue to explore innovative ways to support our team's health and productivity, I've come across a concept that could truly make a positive difference.
>
> The concept is to form a group of movement champions within our organisation. These champions would be dedicated individuals passionate about promoting movement and wellbeing among their colleagues. The goal is to create a community of advocates for movement who inspire and encourage their peers to make small but impactful changes in their daily routines.
>
> I firmly believe that the power of leading by example is invaluable. When employees witness their colleagues embracing healthier habits, they are more likely to follow suit. By gathering a group of enthusiastic movement champions, we can amplify our efforts and foster a culture of wellbeing that extends across departments and levels.
>
> These champions wouldn't need to be fitness experts; rather, they would serve as relatable figures who understand the challenges of a busy workday. They would champion simple initiatives such as incorporating short movement breaks, suggesting accessible desk exercises and even organising fun competitions aimed at enriching employee experience.
>
> I'm reaching out to you with this idea because I value your insights and leadership. Your endorsement and support of this initiative could provide the momentum needed to bring it to

life. I believe that establishing a team of movement champions aligns perfectly with our organisation's commitment to creating a positive and healthy work environment.

If you're interested, I would be thrilled to discuss this idea further and explore how we can put together a group of dedicated movement champions. Their enthusiasm could set the stage for a healthier, more energetic workplace that benefits everyone.

Thank you for considering this proposal. I'm eager to hear your thoughts and explore the potential of forming a team of movement champions to make a lasting impact on our organisation.

Warm regards,

[name]

Know someone who'll make a great movement champion? An email template awaits you at lizziewilliamson.com/active to help you to get them on board!

So, are you prepared to lead change in your workplace? It all begins when a spark of passion unites people who share a common vision and inspires them to take that crucial first step towards a brighter, more active future. Gather your colleagues, secure leadership support and collaborate with like-minded individuals within your organisation. As movement champions, you have a unique role to play in developing a more active and engaging work environment.

Core points

- Movement isn't a nice-to-have; it's an integral part of our shared journey. When colleagues embrace an active workday, they convey the message that taking care of oneself is not just acceptable but encouraged.

- Both leaders and team members can use social influence as a tool for bringing physical activity to their workplaces.
- We need our leaders to not just *say* it's okay but to actually *do it themselves*. Employees want a green light to take those much-needed active breaks and make movement a priority.
- You can start small – stand up, stretch and encourage your colleagues to join you in a brief walk around the office.
- Now it's time to build momentum – consider sending one of my Active Workday emails to your co-workers and form a team of movement champions. Be the change you wish to see!

14

Define your purpose

Laying the foundation for change

Without leaps of imagination or dreaming,
we lose the excitement of possibilities.
Dreaming, after all, is a form of planning.
Gloria Steinem

In this critical phase of the active workday revolution you'll dive deep into the creation of your vision, mission and values. This is the point at which you'll explore the core principles that will guide your mission. This part of the framework is about gaining clarity on the broader picture and setting the foundations for your movement.

People are at the heart of any revolution, and the active workday revolution is no exception. To bring about lasting change, challenge the status quo and reshape your approach to work and wellbeing in the workplace, you must present your colleagues with a compelling vision of what could be. You must also articulate the mission and values that underpin this vision.

This phase is about creating a solid foundation. It's about empowering your colleagues with a clear direction for the future and articulating the core values that will drive your mission. It's a critical step in building a movement with purpose and encouraging your colleagues to unite behind a shared set of principles.

Above and below the waterline: the founding principles of your active workday

You've prepared to execute this part of the framework by conducting thorough research and engaging in open discussions with your team, as we covered in chapter 12. That research isn't just about facts and figures; it's also about understanding the pulse of your organisation so you can construct a well-informed and suitable active workplace foundation comprising your unique vision, mission, values and objectives.

Imagine your active workday framework as an iceberg, with the vision, mission and values deep beneath the waterline, forming the strong foundation of your initiative. Just above the water's surface, you'll find your objectives, representing the measurable goals that mark your progress. Atop the visible peak of the iceberg are the dynamic ideas, steps and plans that everyone gets to witness in action.

By developing both the visible and the hidden principles of your active workday – that is, the whole iceberg – and capping it off with a public-facing movement manifesto, you help to achieve team buy-in to a tailor-made strategy. Ensure that your vision, mission and values align seamlessly with your organisation's broader strategies and goals. This will create a unified sense of purpose.

The big picture: your vision, mission and values

The second phase of the active workday framework is defining your vision, mission, values and objectives. You can embark on this journey independently, guided by your inner visionary, or with a dedicated team of change-makers who share your enthusiasm.

Each of these core principles warrants thoughtful consideration. Select your preferred method of contemplation, whether that involves jotting down notes, engaging in discussions or creating a mind map to articulate and refine each concept. Together, these well-refined principles will form the foundation upon which your active workday movement stands.

Vision: picturing the ideal workplace

Your vision is a beacon that guides your organisation through the darkest of nights. It's a compelling picture of the workplace you dream of, where employees are healthier, happier and more productive. This is what ignites inspiration and fuels the collective imagination en route to a more active tomorrow.

Dream big. Your vision should be aspirational, motivational and aligned with your company's overarching goals. A well-defined vision serves as a source of inspiration for everyone involved.

Here is an example of a vision statement that might be held by a truly active workplace:

> Our vision is to redefine the modern workplace as a hub of active vitality, where health and wellbeing take precedence, productivity coexists with movement and every individual thrives. We aspire to inspire a global movement towards healthier, more active workplaces, setting a new industry standard and making our workplace a source of inspiration and pride.

Mission: charting your path

Your mission is the compass that points you in the right direction, providing clarity and purpose to your journey. It directs your organisation's behaviour and actions – today, tomorrow and beyond.

Your mission complements your vision by outlining the broad 'how' of your journey. It articulates how your company will behave in order to move towards the vision and specifies the rationale for your actions. In essence, it succinctly conveys what your company stands for, what it offers to the world and what underpins its activities

Consider the following mission statement as example of how you might build upon your vision:

> Our mission is to champion the wellbeing of our employees by fostering a culture of continual movement and vitality

in the workplace. Through a supportive environment and opportunities for physical activity, we aim to enhance their health, happiness and productivity. We lead by example, placing our employees' wellbeing at the forefront to drive their personal and professional growth.

Values: guiding principles

Values are the heart and soul of your approach towards an active workplace. They are the core principles and beliefs of your organisation, and they define its character and culture. It's now time to identify the values that will serve as the guiding principles of your organisation's active revolution. These values should reflect its culture and priorities.

Here are five examples of values that align with an active workplace, drawn from a workshop I ran recently with a healthcare company:

1. **Health and wellbeing.** Prioritising the physical and mental health of employees is a fundamental value. An active workday promotes wellbeing, which in turn enhances overall quality of life.
2. **Productivity.** The value of productivity aligns with the knowledge that staying active during the workday can lead to increased efficiency and better work outcomes. It highlights that movement and productivity go hand in hand.
3. **Balance.** Balancing work responsibilities with physical activity is a key value. It emphasises that an active workday can coexist with work commitments, creating a healthier equilibrium between work and life.
4. **Collaboration.** An active workday promotes teamwork and communication through activities such as walking meetings, which enhance collaboration and creative thinking.
5. **Inspiration.** An active workday can inspire colleagues to adopt healthier work habits and improve their overall wellbeing.

Objectives: measurable milestones

Objectives breathe life into your mission, vision and values, turning your active workday big-picture dream into a tangible reality. They answer the question of 'how' by specifying your goals, creating a path that is both evident and quantifiable.

To define clear objectives, first identify the gap between the results of your research findings and your foundational principles – in other words, where your workplace is now in comparison to the active workplace you want it to become. Then, develop specific goals that work to close that gap. These objectives will guide the actions you take to create this movement. The success of your active workday initiative relies on your ability to track and attain these objectives, so it's essential that they are realistic, measurable and time-bound.

For example, your objectives might involve increasing the number of active workday initiatives or programs, achieving a specific percentage uptake in employee participation in active workday activities, reducing sedentary behaviour during work hours or enhancing employee satisfaction and retention rates through your active workday initiatives.

Objectives are markers on your journey to a more active and vibrant workplace, aligned with your vision, mission and values.

Putting it all together

Bringing together a well-crafted vision, mission, values and objectives offers numerous benefits. An inspiring vision serves as a source of motivation for employees, keeping them engaged and committed to the journey. Your mission provides long-term focus, guiding actions that take you towards the realisation of your vision. Values provide a solid foundation for decision-making, ensuring that choices and actions align with your organisation's principles. Objectives act as the stepping stones that bridge the gap between your current state and the vibrant vision you aspire to create. Together, they create alignment and ensure that everyone is working with a shared, active purpose.

These foundational principles contribute to shaping the culture of your workplace, fostering an environment where wellbeing and physical activity are paramount. Now it's time to build upon these foundations and bring your purpose to life!

Your movement manifesto: defining your commitment to an active workplace

Creating a manifesto after establishing your vision, mission and values offers a multitude of benefits. At this point you distil these core elements into powerful statements that encapsulates the essence of your core principles. A manifesto serves as a rallying cry, a reminder of your collective commitment and a source of inspiration on the journey to a more active and energised workday.

Creating a compelling manifesto for becoming an active workplace involves crafting clear and inspiring statements that encapsulate your organisation's vision, mission, values and commitment to meeting your objectives of integrating physical activity into the workday.

A manifesto is a potent communication tool. It takes your active workplace vision, mission, values and objectives, and it condenses them into a concise, easily shareable document. It fosters understanding and buy-in from all parties, ensuring that everyone is on the same page.

Accountability is another critical aspect. A manifesto sets a clear standard against which actions and decisions can be evaluated. It becomes a reference point for assessing whether the organisation and its members are living up to the stated values and principles.

When articulating your manifesto, use clear and concise language. Each statement in your manifesto should be impactful and easy to understand. The goal is to convey your organisation's commitment to an active workplace in a straightforward and compelling way. Your manifesto should be more than just words; it should inspire action. Use powerful language that encourages your team to embrace a culture of movement and wellbeing. Motivate them to actively participate in making your organisation's vision a reality in their daily work routines.

Here's an example you might like to draw from as you construct your own movement manifesto:

> In our workplace, we commit to embracing a culture of activity and vitality. We understand that movement is the key to unlocking our full potential, both personally and professionally.
>
> We prioritise the wellbeing of our team members, recognising that their health and happiness are fundamental to our collective success. We're dedicated to providing an environment that encourages physical activity and a work-life balance that allows for personal growth.
>
> We believe that an active workday provides the foundation for productivity and success. Movement fuels our creativity, enhances our efficiency and fosters dynamic collaboration.
>
> As a team, we inspire one another through our own actions. We lead by example, motivating our colleagues to adopt active work habits and improve their overall wellbeing.
>
> Our commitment to innovation and adaptation ensures we stay open to new ideas and technologies that promote movement. We recognise that embracing change is essential for our growth.
>
> In our daily routines, we prioritise self-care, acknowledging that taking active breaks is an act of self-compassion that preserves our mental and physical wellbeing.
>
> We thrive in motion and find success, fulfillment and growth in our active workdays. We understand that this journey is as vital as the destination.
>
> This manifesto is our collective commitment to a dynamic workday, a testament to our belief in the transformative power of movement in our professional lives. Together, we re-energise our workdays, fostering an environment that encourages wellbeing, productivity and the boundless possibilities that come with an active approach to work.

The next step is to review and refine your manifesto by seeking input from key stakeholders. This will help you to ensure that your message is as effective as possible. After fine-tuning, it's time to proudly share your manifest through various channels, both within your organisation and externally, encouraging team members to embrace and promote it.

The final – and ongoing – step is to bring the manifesto to life in your workplace, demonstrate your commitment through action and make a meaningful impact. This is where you turn words into action and inspire real change.

Core points

- Fuel change with a compelling vision, a mission that guides and well-defined values for your colleagues.
- Imagine your active workday as an iceberg: vision, mission and values form the bedrock, and objectives measure progress.
- Don't forget to incorporate measurable milestones. As we all know, our brains love the thrill or reaching a goal and receiving a reward.
- A manifesto serves as a rallying cry and reminder of your collective commitment and a source of inspiration.

15

Design your roadmap

Your blueprint for an active workplace

All you need is the plan, the road map, and the courage to press on to your destination.

Earl Nightingale

Welcome to the roadmap phase of the active workplace framework! Your journey to transform your workplace into a dynamic, health-focused environment is well underway. In the earlier stages of this framework, you took the active pulse of your organisation, learned about becoming your own role model and defined your compelling core principles and objectives. Now it's time to take these foundational elements and bring them to life. This roadmap will be your blueprint for action, guiding you from the 'what' to the 'how'.

As we set out to design our roadmap across four stages – discovery, idea generation, idea assessment and action planning – I first want to acknowledge that this process may seem like a like a lot of work in your already busy schedule. However, remember the lasting impact this effort will have on everyone. By the end of these sessions, you'll have a comprehensive roadmap that will lead you and your team towards your active workplace vision and objectives. You'll be equipped with the small, actionable steps that will enable you and your colleagues to harness the advantages of an active workday. This roadmap isn't rigid; it's adaptable and responsive to the evolving needs of your organisation.

As you follow your unique roadmap, you'll see your colleagues become healthier, happier and more engaged as their workplace actively supports their wellbeing and success. So, let's dive into creating the roadmap – where dreams become plans and plans become reality.

Preparing for success

Consider your roadmap-building sessions as opportunities to harness the collective wisdom and enthusiasm of your team while also securing their buy-in. Gather your movement champions and enthusiastic colleagues to create the roadmap collaboratively. By seeking diverse insights from different segments of the workforce you'll ensure that the insights, ideas and actions are not only comprehensive but also inclusive, catering to the unique needs and aspirations of your entire team. Each voice in the room is a valuable resource, capable of generating innovative ideas that will shape your active workday roadmap. This inclusive approach will make the journey towards an active workplace even more engaging and successful.

> *'Employee engagement isn't a one-size-fits-all strategy. It's about recognising and utilising the unique strengths and interests of your team members. The goal is to create an environment where every individual feels seen, heard and valued. That's when engagement truly flourishes.' – Sarah*

To prepare for these sessions, you'll also need to gather relevant data from the research phase (including assessments of your organisation's current state and insights from employee feedback) as well as the vision, mission, values and objectives developed in chapter 14. Equipped with this information, your sessions will be well-informed and aligned with your active workplace vision.

Invite participants to the sessions and create a conducive environment for brainstorming and planning. Get your whiteboards, sticky notes and pens ready, ensuring you have all the necessary materials to facilitate the collaborative process. Set up a comfortable space where your team can freely share ideas and build upon one another's insights. With everyone engaged and well-prepared you'll be able to make the most of these discovery, idea-generation, idea-assessment and action-planning sessions and steer your organisation towards a healthier, more active workplace.

Session 1: discovery

In the first session you'll explore the wealth of insights gathered from your research, core principles and objectives. You'll also pinpoint the roadblocks in your path. Participants will gain a comprehensive understanding of your people and organisation's state of play, the big-picture destination and the obstacles you may encounter on the journey.

Where are we going and why?

To kick things off, share the purpose of this session to unite and align your team in a common direction. Together, you'll lay the foundation for the first segment of your roadmap, which will guide your actions and initiatives moving forward.

Next, delve into the compelling reasons why you want to create an active workplace. Emphasise the myriad benefits of movement, both within and beyond the workplace. Chapter 1 provides a comprehensive overview of these reasons, which will serve as a powerful motivation for your active workplace initiative. Encourage participants to share their personal stories and experiences about how physical activity and movement have positively impacted their lives. This personal touch can help create a sense of purpose and motivation among the participants, reinforcing the 'why' behind this transformative journey.

To create a successful roadmap you need to know where you're going, so it's time to share what lies beneath the iceberg of the strategies you'll be creating. This involves painting a vivid picture of the collective vision, mission, values and objectives established in chapter 14. This is crucial for setting the context and ensuring that the outcomes of this session align with the big picture. Don't forget to introduce and discuss your movement manifesto (also covered in chapter 14). This will serve as a guiding document, so provide everyone with a copy or prominently display it on the wall or whiteboard.

Where are we now?

Next, reveal some of the insights gained from the initial research you undertook in the first phase of the active workday framework (see chapter 12). This is your starting point. Share key findings about your workplace's current physical activity levels. Additionally, mention any prevailing attitudes that individuals encounter in their pursuit of an active workday. Open up the discussion for team members to share their own insights.

What's getting in our way?

This is a prime opportunity to transition into a brainstorming session dedicated to identifying roadblocks that may get in the way of you reaching your destination.

On sticky notes or whiteboards, in small groups or as a team, have everyone write down the roadblocks and obstacles that they feel get in the way of an active workday. Encourage honest sharing about challenges such as time constraints, lack of motivation, company culture, physical health and even external factors. For example, here are some roadblocks that have emerged in active workplace brainstorming sessions I've run over the years:

- not enough time, busy schedules, back-to-back meetings and heavy workloads
- feeling tired, negativity, anxiety and old habits

- communication challenges, risk aversion, lack of trust and lack of leadership
- injury and sickness, physical restrictions, personal commitments and environmental factors.

Have everyone place their sticky notes on their group's designated wall or whiteboard and appoint a representative from each group to present these roadblocks to the rest of the team. Encourage all participants to keep these roadblocks in mind in the lead-up to the idea-generating session, reflecting on how they can turn obstacles into opportunities, as discussed in chapter 2.

Session 2: idea generation

The next session begins with some inspiring and collaborative brainstorming, the purpose of which is to unleash ideas that will propel you towards your objective of embracing the active workday and all it entails. It's time to tap into the collective wisdom of your team and harness the power of collaboration.

All ideas are welcome

Begin the idea-generating session with a brief and inspiring review of your active workday ambitions and objectives and the insights gathered from the discovery session. Introduce the session's purpose: to generate ideas for creating and fostering an active workplace. Explain that during this phase, you'll be harnessing the collective intelligence and innovative spirit of the team to come up with the ideas and approaches that will drive the active workday initiative forward. This collaborative endeavour ensures that every team member's input is valuable in shaping your journey towards a more active and productive workplace.

Explain that this is as an opportunity to hear everyone's ideas about making an active workplace a reality, emphasising that no idea is too big, small or silly. Encourage participants to think boldly, creatively and without restraint. It's important to understand that diverse perspectives and novel ideas are highly valued and warmly welcomed. Reveal that the process of assessing and selecting the ideas to move forward with will come in a later session. Encourage open and free thinking. There are no wrong answers. Prioritise quantity over quality during this brainstorming phase to generate as many ideas as possible. Encourage participants to build on each other's ideas to spark creativity.

Brainstorm ideas

Divide into smaller groups, making sure there is a mix of roles, departments and backgrounds within each group to promote diverse thinking and innovative solutions. Choose brainstorming techniques that best fit your team's dynamics – whether that's mind mapping around central themes, using brainstorming games designed to inspire creative thinking or simply holding open discussions.

Provide participants with guiding questions to stimulate their brainstorming process, such as the following:

- How can we encourage physical activity during the workday?
- What movement initiatives could we implement?
- Are there creative ways to incorporate movement into meetings?
- How can we make our workspace more conducive to physical activity?
- What resources and support can we provide to employees?

Set a specific time limit for the brainstorming phase, preferably between 20 and 30 minutes, to maintain energy and focus on generating ideas. In each group, designate a note-taker to capture the generated ideas on a shared document, a whiteboard or sticky notes. Ensure that the ideas are clear and concise.

Here are some ideas that have emerged from active workday sessions I've held before:

- **Buddy system** – encourage accountability and support through partnerships with colleagues.

- **Evidence and reasoning** – address risk aversion with evidence and reasoning for active changes.
- **Movement prompts** – provide reminders to encourage movement throughout the day.
- **Physical activities in meetings** – incorporate physical activities, such as walking, into work meetings.
- **Scheduled movement breaks** – introduce regular breaks to encourage physical activity.
- **Wellness resources** – provide resources for personal wellness, such as movement videos and wellness equipment.
- **Visual reminders** – place visual cues or reminders around the workplace to prompt physical activity and wellness practices.

Select ideas to present

Having brainstormed, it's time for each group to present their ideas to the larger group in a clear and organised manner. These ideas may be documented on a large paper covered in sticky notes, presented on a poster, compiled in a document or displayed on a whiteboard. Ensuring that the ideas are well-documented and accessible is crucial for the next session's effectiveness.

Encourage all groups to openly share their thoughts and contributions. It's important to create an atmosphere where every idea is captured, acknowledged and valued. This collaborative sharing and capturing process sets the stage for evaluating and selecting the most promising concepts to be included in the active workplace roadmap.

By making sure that all ideas are visible and easily accessible, you promote transparency and open dialogue, allowing the entire team to participate in the decision-making process and select the ideas that will shape the future of your active workplace.

Session 3: idea assessment

In the third session you'll evaluate the ideas that have emerged and select those that will form the foundation of your action plan. This is the moment of decision, when you distil your options into a clear path forward.

Organise and present ideas

Welcome everyone to the third session of designing your roadmap, setting the stage that you'll be focusing on the evaluation and selection of the ideas generated in the previous brainstorming session. Take a moment to acknowledge the incredible work generated during the brainstorming session. Go team! It's essential to recognise the collective effort that has brought you to this point.

The generated ideas may be documented on sticky notes, captured as photos of the whiteboard activity or compiled in a document, depending on the method used in the idea-generation session. Appoint someone to organise and present these ideas to the team. They should ensure that each idea is clear and easy to understand.

To streamline the assessment process, consider organising the ideas by grouping similar concepts together. This can help identify patterns, common themes or opportunities to combine ideas for more significant impact.

Assess impact and effort

Collectively assess each idea based on two key factors: its potential impact and the effort required for implementation. Explain how you will use this assessment to make informed decisions and prioritise ideas that align most effectively with your goals and the resources at your disposal.

As a team, consider each idea's expected impact and the effort required for its realisation. For example, beginning meetings with two minutes of moves is likely to offer substantial results with minimal effort. This idea would then be assessed as 'high impact' and 'low effort'. In contrast, making physical activities engaging by gamifying tasks and challenges would be more likely to be assessed as 'high impact' and 'high effort'.

Evaluate shortlist and select ideas to implement

Having assessed each idea according to impact and effort, collectively determine a shortlist of ideas that align best with your goals and available resources. Suggest that the team mainly consider ideas that fall into both the 'high impact' and 'low effort' categories. These ideas are often the most practical and beneficial for implementation, particularly when you're just starting your active workday journey. It's worth noting, however, that sometimes it can be beneficial to choose a 'high impact' and 'high effort' idea to work with too, as despite their demands they can bring about substantial rewards and innovations. Remember, too, that even ideas classified as 'low impact' and 'low effort' can be valuable, as small changes can accumulate and lead to meaningful transformations.

Session 4: action planning

With the selected ideas in hand, it's time for planning. In the fourth session you'll break down the big picture into smaller, actionable steps. These steps will turn your strategy into reality. Get ready to put your plan into action!

Prioritise ideas for implementation

In this session, your first task is to decide which idea from the exercise shortlist to prioritise for implementation. You can do this using a vote or a group discussion and consensus. This collaborative decision ensures that the selected idea has the collective support and commitment of the team, laying the foundations for creating a comprehensive action plan.

Create an action plan

Once the idea is decided upon, get everyone ready for planning time. Celebrate that you've done the necessary steps to ensure what you are taking action on will resonate with your workforce thanks to a thorough research, brainstorming and selection process. This action plan should specify the necessary next steps, the responsible individuals or teams, the timelines for execution, how success will be measured and the resources that will be required. This level of detail is vital and ensures that everyone is on the same page about what needs to be done.

Here is a sample action plan for introducing moves at the start of meetings:

Action plan: introduction and promotion of meeting moves

Objective: to introduce and promote the practice of incorporating brief, two-minute movement activities at the beginning of meetings to enhance team engagement and overall wellbeing.

Responsible party: HR team and wellness committee.

Resources needed: two-minute videos.

Timeline: to be initiated within the next two weeks.

1. **Orientation and training.** Conduct a brief orientation session with the HR team and wellness committee members to explain the purpose and benefits of starting meetings with movement. Ensure they understand the role and significance of this practice.
2. **Develop meeting moves guidelines.** Collaborate with the wellness committee to create a list of simple, accessible and non-disruptive meeting moves. These should be designed to engage team members without causing disruptions.
3. **Engage a movement expert.** Collaborate with a movement expert to create a series of two-minute movement activity videos tailored to the meeting moves idea. The videos should align with the guidelines developed by the wellness committee.
4. **Awareness campaign.** Launch an internal awareness campaign through company communication channels (email, newsletters, intranet and physical posters) to introduce the concept of meeting moves. Include compelling content on the benefits of physical activity for productivity and wellbeing.

5. **Communication with teams.** Reach out to department heads and team leaders to inform them about the new practice. Encourage them to incorporate meeting moves into their team meetings and provide guidelines.
6. **Demonstration sessions.** Organise a series of live or virtual demo sessions for department heads and team leaders to illustrate how meeting moves can be seamlessly integrated into meetings. Address any questions or concerns they may have.
7. **Trial period.** Encourage departments to implement meeting moves on a trial basis for one month. During this time, gather feedback and track the impact on team engagement and wellbeing.
8. **Feedback collection.** Use surveys or feedback sessions to collect input from employees and leaders about their experiences with meeting moves. Understand what worked well and what could be improved.
9. **Analysis and adjustments.** Analyse the feedback and data collected during the trial period. Collaborate with the wellness committee to make any necessary adjustments to the meeting moves to ensure they align with the needs and preferences of different teams.
10. **Roll-out.** After the trial period and necessary adjustments, launch the practice of meeting moves company-wide. Encourage all departments to integrate them into their meetings and foster a culture of active engagement.
11. **Regular check-ins.** Schedule regular check-in sessions with department heads and team leaders to monitor the continued implementation of meeting moves. Address any challenges and provide support as needed.
12. **Performance metrics.** Define key performance metrics to measure the impact of meeting moves, such as increased engagement levels, improved wellbeing and changes in meeting productivity.

What about the rest of your ideas?

You and the team might be wondering about the other great ideas generated during your brainstorming and assessment sessions. Assure everyone that these other ideas won't be forgotten. To begin with you're focusing on one idea to ensure a comprehensive plan is developed. However, make plans to revisit and prioritise the remaining ideas in future action-planning sessions. This phased approach allows you to make steady progress while ensuring that each idea is implemented effectively.

Tips for success

To ensure the success of your idea and action-planning sessions, here are some key considerations to keep in mind throughout your journey.

Make sure everyone is invited

In the pursuit of an active workplace, prioritising inclusivity is essential. When crafting and implementing ideas, it's imperative to accommodate varying needs and consider the diverse requirements of your workforce. This commitment revolves around the belief that every employee should have equal access to opportunities for physical activity. Ensure that your strategies are designed to be adaptable, allowing individuals with different abilities and needs to participate equally.

Accessibility should be a key focus in your approach. Your tactics should intentionally be flexible, recognising that not all employees share the same preferences or capabilities. Encourage individuals to personalise their approach to staying active, be it through desk exercises, walking or more intensive physical activities. Engage with employees, especially those with varying needs, as a core aspect of this strategy. Seek their feedback to ensure that your initiatives meet their specific requirements and allow for the ongoing refinement of strategies and tactics. Remember, inclusivity is more than a buzzword; it's an integral part of the active workplace culture.

Get leadership buy-in

As you embark on the journey to cultivate a workplace culture that champions wellbeing, securing leadership buy-in becomes an imperative. The influence of dedicated champions of wellbeing within the company is undoubtedly valuable, but support from company leadership can take your initiatives to new heights. By gaining the endorsement of your organisation's decision-makers, you send a powerful message: wellbeing is not just a slogan but is integral to your mission, and it significantly impacts the company's growth and success.

As you know from chapter 12, the call for wellbeing in the workplace is more than a trend, and compelling data and research demonstrate its far-reaching advantages. Communicate this research to your leadership team, revealing how the numbers speak for themselves. Let them know about the tangible economic benefits experienced by a thriving workplace that prioritises health.

In organisations that have yet to fully embrace wellbeing, it may fall upon proactive individuals such as yourself to initiate change. This is where being your own role model comes in. Seek out like-minded colleagues who recognise the value of employee wellbeing and form a collective voice that can influence decision-makers. By highlighting the financial, health and productivity benefits of an active workplace, you can show that the investment in wellbeing is not just a moral or ethical consideration but also a strategic and financially sound decision. With compelling data, real-life stories and a well-structured roadmap in hand, you are well-equipped to gain the support needed to foster a vibrant, active and thriving workplace.

Get excited!

By embarking on these roadmap sessions, you're taking a significant step towards fostering a culture of movement, wellbeing and collaboration within your organisation. Your insights and commitment will transform mere ideas into a movement that enriches the lives of individuals and elevates your organisation's collective spirit. You now have a clear action plan with which to steer your people's efforts to create a workplace that not only prioritises health and activity but also serves as a wellspring of pride and motivation for all.

> *'Wow, after today's session I'm seriously pumped up and proud of what we're about to do. This whole movement for a healthier, more active workplace is like a breath of fresh air. I've got this newfound sense of purpose and can't wait to team up with my co-workers as we embark on this exciting journey. We're definitely onto something big!' – Adam*

Core points

- The roadmap is a guide for turning your active workday vision and objectives into reality. It incorporates the ideas and action plans needed to bring your vision to life.
- Though this can feel like a lot of work to add to your already busy schedule, remember the long-term impact for everyone – happier, more productive employees who want to come to work and a happier, more productive workplace for *you*.
- Dive into the discovery, idea-generation, idea-assessment and action-planning sessions for a vibrant and active work culture.
- Inclusivity is essential. It's imperative to accommodate varying needs and consider the diverse requirements of your workforce.
- Demonstrate the strategic and financial benefits of an active workplace using compelling data and real stories to gain buy-in from leadership and decision-makers.

16

Rally your people

The heart of an active workplace

Remember the Bob Dylan rule:
It's not just a record, it's a movement.
Seth Godin

At this point in executing the active workday framework, you've already embarked on an incredible journey to transform your workplace into a thriving hub of health and wellbeing. You've conducted in-depth research to understand the current state of play within your organisation, learned how to be your own leader, outlined a grand vision for the future and charted a clear roadmap to illuminate the path ahead. Now it's time to get your entire team on board, ensuring they not only understand the active workday concept but also wholeheartedly embrace it.

The aim of this phase in the framework is to equip you with the tools and insights needed to make the active workday a long-term reality for your workplace. While leadership buy-in is vital, true transformation comes from individuals within your organisation embracing the active workday. This chapter covers spreading the message throughout your workplace, removing any roadblocks that may hinder your progress and making the journey easy and enjoyable for all. Then, once everyone is informed, engaged and excited, we explore strategies involving friendly competition and challenges to ensure the active workday doesn't fizzle out. These elements will help keep everyone motivated and on track, creating a culture of continuous improvement. Lastly, we focus on the art of celebrating even the smallest of wins, the final piece of the puzzle to seal the deal for your active workplace movement. So, let's get started, harnessing your most valuable resource – your people – to propel your active workplace revolution beyond an idea and into lasting change.

Spreading the word: awareness campaigns and communication

On the journey to establish a healthier, more active workplace, it's crucial to grasp that education and communication are of paramount importance. Even the most compelling vision and comprehensive suite of wellness initiatives will have little effect if you don't ensure that your team comprehends, embraces and actively participates in the transformation of your workplace culture.

The educational journey commences with awareness. This is about providing your team with a clear understanding of why an active workplace is crucial not only for your company's success but also for their personal wellbeing. It's about explaining the profound scientific connection between physical activity and enhanced focus, heightened productivity and overall health. The 'why' behind the active workday becomes the catalyst for change – for revolution – so be sure to educate your team about the significant advantages an active workday can bring to their lives.

Don't stop at the 'why'. Move forward with the 'how' by giving your team the practical knowledge, easy-to-follow strategies and a wealth of resources to make an active workday their new norm. It's all about making it a simple as possible for your colleagues to incorporate physical activity into their daily routines. Remember the desk-friendly chairercise moves from chapter 2 and 'Energise while you boil!' from chapter 5? I've created posters for these sets of micro moves and more for you to download, print and put up in the office. Explore these resources and more at lizziewilliamson.com/active.

You could also organise 'lunch and learns' and workshops where movement champions such as yourself can dive into the link between physical activity and improved work outcomes and share tips for incorporating more movement into the workday. Allow your team to pick the brains of those who have the wisdom to share by creating a space where learning is as interactive as it is informative.

Remember, education isn't one-size-fits-all; every individual is unique in their learning preferences and habits. Some thrive on informative seminars, while others prefer engaging in hands-on activities. Tailor your education to cater to a spectrum of learning styles. This not only ensures that everyone gets the message but also makes it more engaging and enjoyable.

Complement your educational efforts with consistent and robust communication that continuously reinforces the active workday message. Regularly update your team on their progress, share success stories and provide data-backed evidence of the positive impact on workplace dynamics. When you communicate honestly and effectively, you foster a sense of trust and shared commitment.

TRY THIS: email campaigns

To support an active workday transformation, effective communication across a range of workplace platforms – encompassing email, digital tools such as Yammer, group chats and traditional notice boards – is key. Use these to educate, motivate and foster participation in your active workday revolution. Designing engaging content that resonates with your colleagues is essential to driving positive change, so here are some tips for capturing attention and inspiring action:

- **Suggest practical actions.** Ensure your messages include practical actions that are easy for your colleagues to implement. For example, you might feature some quick desk exercises that can be performed during the workday – find lots of ideas in the first two parts of this book or check out the explainer videos at lizziewilliamson.com/active. Make sure the content is actionable and directly applicable in their daily routines.

- **Keep it fun and engaging.** Share (with permission) anecdotes from colleagues who have embraced movement at work and experienced positive changes. Highlight creative movement challenges or friendly competitions that employees have participated in – more on those soon! Create an environment in which colleagues eagerly anticipate your emails as sources of inspiration and entertainment.
- **Share science and research.** Weave in the fascinating science and research behind the benefits of an active workday and offer insights into how regular physical activity enhances cognitive abilities, fuels creativity and contributes to overall wellbeing. Supporting your messages with data and studies adds credibility and encourages participation.

By incorporating these elements into your communications, you can provide colleagues with engaging, actionable and educational content that empowers them to embrace an active workday. Your messages will become valuable assets that enhance their experience at work and contribute to a healthier and more vibrant workplace culture.

Encouraging participation: challenges and friendly competition

Wellness challenges are more than just a workplace pastime – they're an effective strategy for inspiring participation, fostering team spirit and amplifying the impact of your initiative to bring the active workday to your workplace. Think of them as propelling your efforts to the next level. So, why do challenges work so well? Well, it's all about the fun and friendly competition they bring to the table.

When people come together to form teams and set collective goals, something extraordinary happens. It's like unleashing the power of a superhero team, in which every member is striving towards a common goal. Whether the goal is walking a specific number of kilometres as a team, having the highest combined exercise time or simply meeting the benchmark of daily active minutes, competitive spirit takes over. Suddenly, the workplace transforms into an arena of friendly rivalries and encouraging cheers, both in-person and virtually.

Take, for example, step competitions. Here, individuals or teams engage in a lively race to claim the title of the highest step count. Each day becomes an adventure where every step matters. And the best part? It's not about beating others down; it's about lifting each other up. Colleagues motivate and support one another, creating a bond that goes beyond the challenge.

Put active culture shift in the calendar

Wellness challenges offer a refreshing change from the usual office routine. They provide an opportunity for people to break away from their desks, breathe in the fresh air and engage in activities that promote wellbeing. Whether it's the start of a new year, a fresh month or the dawn of the next financial year, seize these 'fresh starts' as the perfect moments to kickstart a wellness challenge.

You can also maximise the impact of globally celebrated days, weeks and months. These themed periods offer ideal opportunities to align movement challenges or competitions with specific health, wellbeing and awareness initiatives. They provide a chance to turn your workplace into an arena of inspiration, excitement and healthy competition – all while making strides towards a happier, more active and thriving work environment.

Here are just a few key events and suggestions for how you might engage with each in your workplace:

- **International Day of Happiness – 20 March**
  Spread joy through movement challenges that boost mood and happiness.
- **World Health Day – 7 April**
  Launch comprehensive wellness challenges that encompass physical, mental and social wellbeing.

- **R U OK Day – second Thursday in September**
  Group walks, meditation sessions and team-building exercises can serve as great initiatives to emphasise the importance of checking in on colleagues and asking, 'Are you okay?'
- **National Safe Work Month – October**
  Focus on workplace safety through movement challenges that encourage ergonomic practices and regular breaks.

Now, take action! Look at your next six months and plan two wellbeing challenges. For more information on important dates and to download a comprehensive wellbeing calendar, visit lizziewilliamson.com/active.

TRY THIS: the 21-day challenge

Whether you're just starting your active workday revolution or you've noticed commitment waning, a 21-day challenge can be a super effective solution, complete with a clear framework and timeline. By committing to a specific action for 21 days and framing it as a challenge, you tap into the power of small wins and friendly competition to build momentum.

You can initiate your own 21-day challenge by following the sample provided here or visit lizziewilliamson.com/active to join one I've already set up – together, we can make this transformation even more rewarding!

The 21-day movement habit kickstart!

Ready to spark positive change and embrace a healthier, more active you? Join us for the exhilarating 21-day movement habit kickstart! This challenge empowers you to pick a single movement habit and commit to it every day for three weeks. Get ready to transform your routine and infuse your days with vitality.

How it works:

1. *Choose your habit.* Select one movement habit that resonates with you. Whether it's a daily walk, a quick stretch routine, a mini dance break or something entirely unique, this is your chance to make movement a joyful part of your day.
2. *Commit.* For 21 days, dedicate a few minutes to your chosen movement habit every day. Consistency is key, so no matter how busy life gets, prioritise this empowering practice.
3. *Celebrate your progress.* Each day you complete your chosen movement habit, mark it off on the tracker provided. Celebrate your dedication and progress!

Why you should join:

- *To boost wellbeing.* Experience the benefits of consistent movement, from increased energy to reduced stress.
- *To build habits.* Cultivate a positive habit that becomes an integral part of your daily routine.
- *To feel accomplished.* Celebrate your commitment and growth as you conquer the 21-day kickstart.
- *To grow community support.* Connect with fellow participants, share experiences and inspire each other along the way.

Dates: [Enter your dates here.]

How to join:

- Sign up at [enter your registration link here or join my challenge at lizziewilliamson.com/active].
- Receive your movement habit tracker and additional resources.
- Embark on your 21-day movement journey and inspire others with your dedication!

Prizes and recognition:

Participate actively and share your progress on the company platform to be entered in the draw to win exciting prizes.

Don't miss this incredible opportunity to ignite positive change and create lasting active workday habits. Let's embrace the 21-day movement habit kickstart and celebrate the joy of moving together!

Let's move, thrive and celebrate together!

Be sure to infuse challenges with elements that keep participants engaged and motivated. For example, if your team loves going to the movies, you might make the prize a double pass to a posh cinema plus a voucher for the concession stand. If they could use a little extra encouragement, consider whether a weekly draw of smaller prizes might help.

Sealing the deal: celebrate and reward

Let's keep the revolution going! With your roadmap in hand, leadership support and accountability systems in place, education well underway, clear communication channels set and some friendly competition on the horizon, it's time to revisit a pivotal concept: the power of celebration in closing the habit loop and solidifying change.

As we explored in chapter 4, the key to making any active change stick is turning it into a habit – and the secret sauce for habit formation is closing the loop with reward and celebration. Here are some strategies for this important and joyful part of your active workday journey:

- Acknowledge and celebrate every small achievement, be it a personal fitness milestone, a colleague's step goal or the whole team's consistent use of meeting moves.
- Highlight achievements resulting from your active workday initiative as a whole. Invite team members to share success stories, testimonials and before-and-after stories illustrating how movement enhances teamwork, collaboration and the overall office atmosphere.

- Create a system for team members to nominate their peers for their efforts in promoting movement. Regularly recognise and celebrate those who inspire movement, boosting their morale and setting positive examples for others to follow.
- Feature employees who have been outstanding advocates for the active workday movement. Share their stories and insights to inspire others and demonstrate the tangible benefits of incorporating movement into the work routine.

TRY THIS: Movement Mondays

As you know, consistency is key to sustaining an active workplace culture. To keep the enthusiasm and energy alive week after week – and for plenty of opportunities to close the habit loop with celebration – try introducing 'Movement Mondays' as a regular event. This will ensure that movement remains an enduring part of your work routine, making it accessible to all employees no matter how packed their schedules may be, and gives you weekly opportunities for celebration.

Here's how it works. Every Monday, encourage your team to include at least one moment of movement in their workday. It can be as simple as scheduling a walking meeting, squeezing in a brief chair stretch or even having an office dance-off. The idea is to provide flexibility and adaptability to accommodate all employees' responsibilities and preferences.

After they've participated in their chosen movement, invite everyone to share their experiences with their colleagues. They can do this on internal social platforms, in a team meeting or in a designated space within your workplace, such as a bulletin board or a digital hub. By sharing these moments, you foster a sense of unity and togetherness, motivating others to join in and make active workdays an enduring part of the work culture.

By integrating Movement Mondays as a routine event, you ensure that the spirit of celebration and activity remains a consistent part of your workplace. This approach makes maintaining an active workday a sustainable and enjoyable endeavour for all.

Look how far you've come!

As you come to the end of the active workday framework, I want to celebrate a vital person in this process – YOU! Whether you realise it or not, the fact you have reached the end of this book means that you are committed to change and you've taken the first steps to make it happen.

You – yes, you – are an active workplace champion, and even if you can only implement a fraction of the guidance from this book, you are a pivotal part of the active workplace movement. For that I appreciate and applaud you.

Think of where – and who – you were when you first picked up this book. Pause and acknowledge any changes you've made, big or small, to begin to rethink your workday, change the system and prioritise wellbeing. Have you found yourself incorporating movement breaks into your workday? Maybe it's becoming automatic and you're starting to prioritise wellness in the workplace without even having to think about it. That's a reason to feel excited.

Whatever shift to your workday ethos has been inspired by *The Active Workday Advantage*, I want to celebrate you. Change isn't easy. Being seen by people as you make that change can be even harder. Remember, you're not just doing this as a personal project; you're part of an active revolution. Trust that every day, in small ways, you are making better decisions for both your body and your mind – and the effects of those decisions will ripple through your workplace and beyond.

Core points

- Education and communication are the bedrock upon which your active workday success is built.

- Transparency and open dialogue play a pivotal role in an active workplace.
- Use the thrill of (friendly!) competition to your advantage. Take a look at your calendar for the next six months and plan two wellness challenges.
- Rev up your workplace with Movement Mondays – your weekly dose of active, united celebration.
- Ignite inspiration by acknowledging victories, sharing success stories and spotlighting movement advocates, fostering an active, inspired workplace culture.

The next steps

This is your moment to choose. Do you let this book gather dust on your bookshelf, forgotten and abandoned? Do you allow the opportunity to transform your work life to slip through your fingers? Or do you seize this moment, this golden opportunity to change the way you work and revolutionise your life? Do you take action and become the architect of your own success, using the power of movement to your advantage? The choice is yours, and it's a choice that can make all the difference.

By choosing to take action, you're not just making a personal commitment; you're also joining the active workday movement to care for your physical and mental wellbeing at work. This is a movement in which you will thrive, where you'll prioritise your health and happiness with the understanding that the two are inseparable.

When you take the simple step of breaking up your workday with movement, you're doing yourself a favour. You're also sending a powerful message to those around you. You're telling your colleagues, your friends, your family and even strangers that it's okay to take care of themselves too. You're granting them permission to be the best versions of themselves.

Your small, seemingly insignificant actions catalyse a chain reaction. Your decision to embrace an active workday inspires others to do the same. Your newfound vitality spreads like wildfire. The person next to you sees your transformation and decides to join the movement too. Soon, the entire office, your entire community, will be swept up in the momentum of change – all because you chose to act.

So, I implore you, do not let this opportunity slip away. Embrace the active workday advantage. Be the beacon of change in your workplace, your community and your life. Choose to take action, become a part of this transformative movement and help others find their path to a better, healthier and happier workday.

Together we can create a world in which everyone enjoys the benefits of an active workday. Together we can change the way we work and live. The power is in your hands and the choice is yours. Join me. Let's make the active workday the new standard for success, fulfillment and happiness.

As you apply the principles from this book, I have no doubt that you will reap the rewards of an active workday advantage. With renewed energy, boundless possibilities and a heart full of vitality, go forth and conquer your workday – and life – like never before. The world is waiting for the best version of you, and that version is always in motion, always thriving. It's got the active workday advantage.

Acknowledgements

Writing a book is a lot like going on a rollercoaster ride. There are moments of sheer elation when your creativity is soaring and you feel on top of the world. But, of course, there are also those dips when self-doubt creeps in and you're gripping the safety bar, wondering why you signed up for this in the first place. It's not something you want to tackle alone.

First and foremost, I owe a huge debt of gratitude to Major Street Publishing, who stamped my ticket and allowed me to hop on board. Working with this fantastic publishing house has been a dream experience and I couldn't have asked for a better team, including Lesley Williams, Will Allen, Eleanor Reader, Patricia Amarilli, Kerry Milin, Tess McCabe and, last but not least, Lauren Mitchell. I took Lauren, my editor extraordinaire, on quite the ride with all my changes and she didn't flinch. Her feedback, support, edits and encouragement made this book so much better.

My book coach and fellow author Amy Molloy proved to be a bona fide rollercoaster expert. Our many hours of 'walk and talks' on the phone really showed that problems are best solved while walking. Amy's writing and editing genius and holistic book coaching were like having a secret weapon on board, helping me navigate through this tumultuous ride. Every time I wanted to scream, 'Stop the ride, I want to get off!', Amy kept me on track.

My good friend Sarah Collier jumped on the rollercoaster too, offering her business strategy prowess and expertise, as she has generously done for me since I started my business. I couldn't include all her wisdom in this book, but it's safely stored away for the next ride.

Thank you to the team at Hachette for not only turning on your cameras and dancing with me on our first virtual meeting, but also for taking this book to booksellers. Thank you also to Jade Warne for the fabulous photo on the back cover, as well as Holly Rayner for the gorgeous hair and make up magic. Shout out to the endorsers who provided social proof and to everyone promoting and selling this book – you're the ones providing fuel for this message and I'm so grateful.

I also greatly appreciate everyone who shared with me their insights on how an active workday has put them and their organisations at an advantage. A heartfelt thank you to all the incredible champions at workplaces and event companies who have trusted me to share my message with their people and audiences. These opportunities have really helped shaped the ideas in this book into something I'm extremely proud of.

Since my first book, *Two Minute Moves*, I've built a community of people who embrace the philosophy of incorporating little moments of movement into their days. The comments, feedback and videos they share of their moves make my day and are wonderful sources of inspiration.

To my cheerleaders – you know who you are – your support has been electrifying. All the conversations, dinners, messages, jogs and walking phone calls to cheer me on have kept me going when I've wanted to stop.

I was lucky enough to have a dad who taught me to dream big and a mum who continues to remind me of the power of taking small steps; these lessons have truly shaped my work and this book. (I wouldn't be here without you, Mum!) My sister, Kate Fell, has been a wellspring of wisdom during our phone calls and my 'don't cry alone' go-to. Both my sister and my brother, Matt Fell, are immense sources of inspiration for me through the extraordinary work they do.

My cats, Connie and Fuji, deserve a mention for their cuddles and patience as their fur-mama constantly interrupted their cozy lap time while practising what she preaches and regularly breaking up long hours of writing with movement.

My hubbie, Felix Williamson, played the role of ground control as I was riding this whirlwind rollercoaster to deadline, supplying the essential items for my survival – food, water and clean clothes – to ensure I didn't descend into complete authorly chaos. I wanted to get a t-shirt printed with 'Thank you so much' on it because I was saying it to him so often. Felix has been the wind beneath my wings for over two decades, constantly encouraging me to dream big and fly high.

Lastly, to my two incredible daughters, Stella and Ruby – my biggest cheerleaders of all. I know they'll be counting the mentions of their names in the book so they can say they're the favourite so – Stella, Stella – now it's even. Their cheers of 'Keep going, Mum!' and 'You've got this!' gave me the courage and determination to ride the rollercoaster to the very end and get this book into your hands, which makes it a journey well worth taking.

About the author

Dubbed by the US media as 'the excuse-buster from Down Under', Lizzie Williamson is the founder and author of *Two Minute Moves* and a TEDx speaker, keynote speaker, fitness presenter and certified personal trainer. She is a regular on morning television and in global news publications, and her work has been featured on *Good Morning America*, *Studio 10*, *The Today Show*, *Women's Health* and *Prevention Magazine*. Through her fun, interactive keynotes, workshops and videos, Lizzie motivates workforces worldwide to integrate movement breaks into their days so they can be their most engaged, energised and happiest selves. She has had thousands of people around the world stretching, moving and dancing at conferences featuring President Barack Obama, Michelle Obama, Arianna Huffington and the Dalai Lama.

Find Lizzie online here:

Instagram – @EnergizeWithLizzie
LinkedIn – linkedin.com/in/lizzie-williamson
TikTok – @EnergizeWithLizzie
YouTube – @EnergizeWithLizzie
lizziewilliamson.com

Resources and references

Exercise can't fix everything, and it's important to reach out for professional support when necessary.

If you're in Australia, you can access 24-hour confidential counselling and crisis support through Lifeline. Call 13 11 14, text 0477 131 114 or visit lifeline.org.au/crisischat.

Elsewhere in the world, search online for the equivalent in your country.

Chapter 1 | The reasons

Bathina, S & Das, UN, 'Brain-derived neurotrophic factor and its clinical implications', *Archives of Medical Science*, vol. 11, no. 6, 2015, pp. 1164–1178.

Carhart, RL & Nutt, DJ, 'Serotonin and brain function: A tale of two receptors', *Journal of Psychopharmacology*, vol. 31, no. 9, 2017, pp. 1091–1120.

Carter, MI & Hinton, PS, 'Physical activity and bone health', *Missouri Medicine*, vol. 111, no. 1, 2014, pp. 59–64.

Chau, JY, Grunseit, AC, Chey, T, Stamatakis, E, Brown, WJ, Matthews, CE, Bauman, AE & van der Ploeg, HP, 'Daily sitting time and all-cause mortality: A meta-analysis', *PLoS One*, vol. 8, no. 11, 2013.

Daneshmandi, H, Choobineh, A, Ghaem, H & Karimi, M, 'Adverse effects of prolonged sitting behavior on the general health of office workers', *Journal of Lifestyle Medicine*, vol. 7, no. 2, 2017.

Diaz, KM, Howard, VJ, Hutto, B, Colabianchi, N, Vena, JE, Safford, MM, Blair, SN & Hooker, SP, 'Patterns of sedentary behavior and mortality in U.S. middle-aged and older adults: A national cohort study', *Annals of Internal Medicine*, vol. 167, no. 7, 2017, pp. 465–475.

Distefano, G & Goodpaster, BH, 'Effects of exercise and aging on skeletal muscle', *Cold Spring Harbor Perspectives in Medicine*, vol. 8, no. 3, 2018, a029785.

Faienza, MF, Lassandro, G, Chiarito, M, Valente, F, Ciaccia, L & Giordano, P, 'How physical activity across the lifespan can reduce the impact of bone ageing: A literature review', *International Journal of Environmental Research and Public Health*, vol. 17, no. 6, 2020, p. 1862.

Farrell, C & Turgeon, DR, 'Normal versus chronic adaptations to aerobic exercise', StatPearls, 29 May 2023, ncbi.nlm.nih.gov/books/NBK572066.

Fleck, SJ & Falkel, JE, 'Value of resistance training for the reduction of sports injuries', *Sports Medicine*, vol. 3, no. 1, 1986, pp. 61–68.

Golen, T & Ricciotti, H, 'Does exercise really boost energy levels?', Harvard Health Publishing, 1 July 2021, health.harvard.edu/exercise-and-fitness/does-exercise-really-boost-energy-levels.

Grant, A, 'There's a name for the blah you're feeling: It's called languishing', *The New York Times*, 19 April 2021, nytimes.com/2021/04/19/well/mind/covid-mental-health-languishing.html.

Harber, VJ & Sutton, JR, 'Endorphins and exercise', *Sports Medicine*, vol. 1, no. 2, 1984, pp. 154–171.

Hong, AR & Kim, SW, 'Effects of resistance exercise on bone health', *Endocrinology and Metabolism*, vol. 33, no. 4, 2018, pp. 435–444.

Hughes, DC, Ellefsen, S & Baar, K, 'Adaptations to Endurance and Strength Training', *Cold Spring Harbor Perspectives in Medicine*, vol. 8, no. 6, 2018.

Hwang, C-L, Chen, S-H, Chou, C-H, Grigoriadis, G, Liao, T-C, Fancher, IS, Arena, R & Phillips, SA, 'The physiological benefits of sitting less and moving more', *Progress in Cardiovascular Disease*, vol. 73, 2022, pp. 61–66.

Kirwan, JP, Sacks, J & Nieuwoudt, S, 'The essential role of exercise in the management of type 2 diabetes', *Cleveland Clinic Journal of Medicine*, vol. 84, no. 7, 2017, S15–S21.

Langhammer, B, Bergland, A & Rydwik, E, 'The importance of physical activity exercise among older people', *BioMed Research International*, vol. 2018, 2018, 7856823.

Levine, JA, *Get Up! Why your chair is killing you and what you can do about it*, Palgrave Macmillan, London, 2015.

Marques, A, Marconcin, P, Werneck, AO, Ferrari, G, Gouveia, ÉR, Kliegel, M, Peralta, M & Ihle, A, 'Bidirectional association between physical activity and dopamine across adulthood: A systematic review', *Brain Sciences*, vol. 11, no. 7, 2021, p. 829.

Matei, D, Trofin, D, Iordan, DA, Onu, I, Condurache, I, Ionite, C & Buculei, I, 'The endocannabinoid system and physical exercise', *International Journal of Molecular Sciences*, vol. 24, no. 3, 1989.

Moghetti, P, Bacchi, E, Brangani, C, Donà, S & Negri, C, 'Metabolic effects of exercise', *Frontiers of Hormone Research*, vol. 47, 2016, pp. 44–57.

National Heart, Lung, and Blood Institute, 'Physical Activity and Your Heart: Benefits', 24 March 2022, nhlbi.nih.gov/health/heart/physical-activity/benefits.

Numakawa, T, Odaka, H & Adachi, N, 'Actions of brain-derived neurotrophic factor and glucocorticoid stress in neurogenesis', *International Journal of Molecular Science*, vol. 18, no. 11, 2017, p. 2312.

Nystoriak, MA & Bhatnagar, A, 'Cardiovascular effects and benefits of exercise', *Frontiers in Cardiovascular Medicine*, vol. 5, no. 135, 2018.

Owen, N, Healy, GN, Matthews, CE & Dunstan, DW, 'Too much sitting: The population health science of sedentary behavior', *Exercise Sport Science Review*, vol. 38, no. 3, 2010.

Park, JH, Moon, JH, Kim, HJ, Kong, MH & Oh, YH, 'Sedentary lifestyle: Overview of updated evidence of potential health risks', *Korean Journal of Family Medicine*, vol. 41, no. 6, 2020, pp. 365–373.

Patel, H, Alkhawam, H, Madanieh, R, Shah, N, Kosmas, CE & Vittorio, TJ, 'Aerobic vs anaerobic exercise training effects on the cardiovascular system', *World Journal of Cardiology*, vol. 9, no. 2, 2017, pp. 134–138.

Pears, M, Kola-Palmer, S & De Azevedo, LB, 'The impact of sitting time and physical activity on mental health during COVID-19 lockdown', *Sport Science Health*, vol. 18, no. 1, 2022.

Raichlen, DA & Alexander, GE, 'Adaptive capacity: An evolutionary neuroscience model linking exercise, cognitive and brain health', *Trends in Neurosciences*, vol. 40, no. 7, 2017, pp. 408–421.

Reggiani, C & Schiaffino, S, 'Muscle hypertrophy and muscle strength: Dependent or independent variables? A provocative review', *European Journal of Translational Myology*, vol. 30, no. 3, 2020, 9311.

Sleiman, SF, Henry, J, Al-Haddad, R, El Hayek, L, Abou Haidar, E, Stringer, T, Ulja, D, Karuppagounder, SS, Holson, EB, Ratan, RR, Ninan, I & Chao, MV, 'Exercise promotes the expression of brain derived neurotrophic factor (BDNF) through the action of the ketone body β-hydroxybutyrate', *eLife*, vol, 5, 2016, e15092.

Sprouse-Blum AS, Smith G, Sugai D & Parsa FD, 'Understanding endorphins and their importance in pain management', *Hawaii Medical Journal*, vol. 69, no. 3, 2010, pp. 70–71.

Suzuki, W, 'The brain-changing benefits of exercise', *TED*, November 2017, ted.com/talks/wendy_suzuki_the_brain_changing_benefits_of_exercise.

Young, SN, 'How to increase serotonin in the human brain without drugs', *Journal of Psychiatry & Neuroscience*, vol. 32, no. 6, 2017, pp. 394–399.

Yüksel, O, Ateş, M, Kızıldağ, S, Yüce, Z, Koç, B, Kandiş, S, Güvendi, G, Karakılıç, A, Gümüş, H & Uysal, N, 'Regular aerobic voluntary exercise increased oxytocin in female mice: The cause of decreased anxiety and increased empathy-like behaviors', *Balkan Medical Journal*, vol. 36, no. 5, 2019, pp. 257–262.

Zunner, BEM, Wachsmuth, NB, Eckstein, ML, Scherl, L, Schierbauer, JR, Haupt, S, Stumpf, C, Reusch, L & Moser, O, 'Myokines and resistance training: A narrative review', *International Journal of Molecular Sciences*, vol. 23, no. 7, 2022, p. 3501.

Chapter 2 | The roadblocks

Ahmadi, MN, Clare, PJ, Katzmarzyk, PT, del Pozo Cruz, B, Lee, IM, Stamatakis, E, 'Vigorous physical activity, incident heart disease, and cancer: how little is enough?', *European Heart Journal*, vol. 43, no. 46, 2022, pp. 4801–4814.

Biswas, A, Oh, PI, Faulkner, GE, Bajaj, RR, Silver, MA, Mitchell, MS & Alter, DA, 'sedentary time and its association with risk for disease incidence, mortality, and hospitalization in adults: A systematic review and meta-analysis', *Annals of Internal Medicine*, vol. 162, 2015, pp. 123–132.

Columbia University Irving Medical Center, 'Rx for prolonged sitting: A five-minute stroll every half hour', ScienceDaily, 12 January 2023, sciencedaily.com/releases/2023/01/230112134726.htm.

Edith Cowan University, 'No time to exercise? What about three seconds a day?', 7 February 2022, ecu.edu.au/newsroom/articles/research/no-time-to-exercise-what-about-three-seconds-a-day.

Harvard Health Publishing, 'Why you should move – even just a little – throughout the day', 14 July 2023, health.harvard.edu/heart-health/why-you-should-move-even-just-a-little-throughout-the-day.

Lieberman, D, *Exercised: The science of physical activity, rest and health*, Penguin, New York, 2021.

Statista, 'Health & fitness clubs – statistics & facts', 30 August 2023, statista.com/topics/1141/health-and-fitness-clubs/#topicOverview.

University of Sydney, 'One-minute bursts of activity during daily tasks could prolong your life, finds study', 9 December 2022, sydney.edu.au/news-opinion/news/2022/12/09/one-minute-bursts-of-activity-during-daily-tasks-could-prolong-y.html.

World Health Organization, Eastern Mediterranean Region, 'Promoting Physical Activity', accessed 27 October 2023, emro.who.int/health-education/physical-activitiy/promoting-physical-activity/What-is-the-recommended-amount-of-exercise.html.

Chapter 3 | Don't wait for motivation

Gilbert, E, *Big Magic: Creative living beyond fear*, Bloomsbury, Sydney, 2016.

Harvard Health Publishing, 'Exercise is an all-natural treatment to fight depression', 2 February 2021, health.harvard.edu/mind-and-mood/exercise-is-an-all-natural-treatment-to-fight-depression.

Pressfield, S, *The War of Art: Break through the blocks and win your creative battles*, Black Irish Entertainment, New York, 2002.

World Health Organization, *Global Action Plan on Physical Activity 2018–2030: More active people for a heavier world*, World Health Organization, Geneva, 2018.

World Health Organization, 'Physical activity', accessed 27 October 2023, who.int/health-topics/physical-activity who.int/health-topics/physical-activity.

Chapter 4 | The path to lasting change

Dwyer, T, Pezic, A, Sun, C, Cochrane, J, Venn, A, Srikanth, V, Jones, G, Shook, R, Sui, X, Ortaglia, A, Blair, S, Ponsonby, A-L, 'Objectively measured daily steps and subsequent long term all-cause mortality: The tasped prospective cohort study', *PLoS One*, vol. 10, no. 12, e0146202.

Fogg, BJ, *Tiny Habits*, accessed 27 October 2023, tinyhabits.com.

Lally, P, van Jaarsveld, CHM, Potts, HWW & Wardle, J, 'How are habits formed: Modelling habit formation in the real world', *European Journal of Social Psychology*, vol. 40, no. 6, 2010, pp. 998–1009.

Lewis, RG, Florio, E, Punzo, D & Borrelli, E, 'The brain's reward system in health and disease', *Advances in Experimental Medicine and Biology*, vol. 1344, 2021, pp. 57–69.

Maxwell, JC, *Success: One day at a time*, Thomas Nelson, New York, 2000.

Robbins, M, *The High 5 Habit: Take control of your life with one simple habit*, Hay House, Carlsbad, 2021.

Chapter 5 | The right environment

Edwards, MK & Loprinzi, PD, 'Experimental effects of brief, single bouts of walking and meditation on mood profile in young adults', *Health Promotion Perspectives*, vol. 8, no. 3, 2018, pp. 171–178.

Wood, W, *Good Habits, Bad Habits: The science of making positive changes that stick*, Pan Macmillan UK, London, 2021.

Chapter 6 | Activate your brain

Aga, K, Inamura, M, Chen, C, Hagiwara, K, Yamashita, R, Hirotsu, M, Seki, T, Takao, A, Fujii, Y, Matsubara, T & Nakagawa, S, 'The effect of acute aerobic exercise on divergent and convergent thinking and its influence by mood', *Brain Sciences*, vol. 11, no. 5, 2021, p. 546.

Albulescu, P, Macsinga, I, Rusu, A, Sulea, C, Bodnaru, A & Tulbure, BT, '"Give me a break!": A systematic review and meta-analysis on the efficacy of micro-breaks for increasing well-being and performance', *PLoS One*, vol. 17, no. 8, 2022, e0272460.

Ariga, A & Lleras, A, 'Brief and rare mental "breaks" keep you focused: Deactivation and reactivation of task goals preempt vigilance decrements', *Cognition*, vol. 118, no. 3, 2011, pp. 439–443.

Bode, C (ed.), *The Portable Thoreau*, Penguin, New York, 1947.

Kim, S, Park, Y & Headrick, L, 'Daily micro-breaks and job performance: General work engagement as a cross-level moderator', *Journal of Applied Psychology*, vol. 103 no. 7, 2018, pp. 772–786.

Ko, YW, Kim, SM, Kang, KD & Han, DH, 'Changes in functional connectivity between default mode network and attention network in response to changes in aerobic exercise intensity', *Psychiatry Investigation*, vol. 20, no. 1, 2023, pp. 27–34.

Kolb, A, *The Upward Spiral: Using neuroscience to reverse the course of depression, one small change at a time*, New Harbinger Publications, Oakland, 2015.

O'Mara, S, *In Praise of Walking: The new science of how we walk and why it's good for us*, WW Norton & Co, New York, 2021.

Rominger, C, Fink, A, Weber, B., Papousek, I & Schwerdtfeger, AR, 'Everyday bodily movement is associated with creativity independently from active positive affect: A Bayesian mediation analysis approach', *Scientific Reports*, vol. 10, 2020, 11985.

Sievertsen, HH, Gino, F & Piovesan, M, 'Cognitive fatigue influences students' performance on standardized tests', *PNAS*, vol. 113, no. 10, 2016, pp. 2621–2624.

Wong, M, 'Stanford study finds walking improves creativity', Stanford News, 24 April 2014, news.stanford.edu/2014/04/24/walking-vs-sitting-042414.

WorkLab, 'Research Proves Your Brain Needs Breaks', Microsoft, 20 April 2021, microsoft.com/en-us/worklab/work-trend-index/brain-research.

Chapter 7 | Change your mind

Caillet, A, Hirshberg, J & Petti, S, 'How your state of mind affects your performance', *Harvard Business Review*, 8 December 2014, hbr.org/2014/12/how-your-state-of-mind-affects-your-performance.

Cuddy, A, 'Your body language may shape who you are', TED, June 2012, ted.com/talks/amy_cuddy_your_body_language_may_shape_who_you_are.

Emmons, RA & McCullough, ME, 'Counting blessings versus burdens: An experimental investigation of gratitude and subjective well-being in daily life', *Journal of Personality and Social Psychology*, vol. 84, no. 2, 2003, pp. 377–389.

Grant, AM & Gino, F, 'A little thanks goes a long way: Explaining why gratitude expressions motivate prosocial behavior', *Journal of Personality and Social Psychology*, vol. 98, no. 6, 2010, pp. 946–955.

Kolb, A, *The Upward Spiral: Using neuroscience to reverse the course of depression, one small change at a time*, New Harbinger Publications, Oakland, 2015.

Progovac, AM, Donohue, JM, Matthews, KA, Chang, C-CH, Habermann, EB, Kuller, LH, Saquib, J, LaMonte, MJ, Salmoirago-Blotcher, E, Zaslavsky, O & Tindle, HA, 'Optimism predicts sustained vigorous physical activity in postmenopausal women', *Preventive Medicine Reports*, vol. 8, 2017, pp. 286–293.

Van Cappellen, P, Edwards, M & Shiota, MN, 'Shades of expansiveness: Postural expression of dominance, high-arousal positive affect, and warmth', *Emotion*, vol. 23, no. 4, 2023, pp. 973–985.

Van Cappellen, P, Ladd, KL, Cassidy, S, Edwards, ME & Fredrickson, BL, Bodily feedback: expansive and upward posture facilitates the experience of positive affect', *Cognition and Emotion*, vol. 36, no. 7, 2022, pp. 1327–1342.

Chapter 8 | Take care of your body

Chatchawan, U, Jupamatangb, U, Chanchitc, S, Puntumetakul, R, Donpunha, W & Yamauchi, J, 'Immediate effects of dynamic sitting exercise on the lower back mobility of sedentary young adults', *Journal of Physical Therapy Science*, vol. 27, no. 11, pp. 3359–3363.

Kim, S, Choi, JY, Moon, S, Park, DH, Kwak, HB & Kang, JH, 'Roles of myokines in exercise-induced improvement of neuropsychiatric function', *Pflugers Archiv*, vol. 471, no. 3, 2019, pp. 491–505.

McGonigal, K, *The Joy of Movement: How exercise helps us find happiness, hope, connection and courage*, Penguin, New York, 2021.

Momma, H, Kawakami, R, Honda, T & Sawada, SS, 'Muscle-strengthening activities are associated with lower risk and mortality in major non-communicable diseases: a systematic review and meta-analysis of cohort studies', *British Journal of Sports Medicine*, vol. 56, no. 13, 2022, pp. 755–763.

Oakman, J, Kinsman, N, Lambert, K, Stuckey, R, Graham, M & Weale, V, 'Working from home in Australia during the COVID-19 pandemic: Cross-sectional results from the Employees Working From Home (EWFH) study', *BMJ Open*, vol. 12, e052733.

Pilates, JH & Miller, WJ, *Return to Life Through Contrology*, Presentation Dynamics, Moscow, 2012.

Radwan, A, Barnes, L, DeResh, R, Englund, C & Gribanoff, S, 'Effects of active microbreaks on the physical and mental well-being of office workers: A systematic review', *Cogent Engineering*, vol. 9, no. 1, 2022, 2026206.

Chapter 9 | Improve your mood

Karageorghis, CI, Priest, DL, Williams, L, Hirani, RM, Lannon, KM & Bates, BJ, 'Ergogenic and psychological effects of synchronous music during circuit-type exercise', *Psychology of Sport and Exercise*, vol. 11, no. 6, 2010, pp. 551–559.

Merom, D, Ding, D & Stamatakis, E 'Dancing participation and cardiovascular disease mortality: A pooled analysis of 11 population-based British cohorts', *American Journal of Preventive Medicine*, vol. 50, no. 6, 2016, pp. 756–760.

Chapter 10 | Vitalise your energy

Albulescu, P, Macsinga, I, Rusu, A, Sulea, C, Bodnaru, A & Tulbure, BT, '"Give me a break!": A systematic review and meta-analysis on the efficacy of micro-breaks for increasing well-being and performance', *PLoS One*, vol. 17, no. 8, 2022, e0272460.

Bergouignan, A, Legget, KT, De Jong, N, Kealey, E, Nikolovski, J, Groppel, JL, Jordan, C, O'Day, R, Hill, JO & Bessesen DH, 'Effect of frequent interruptions of prolonged sitting on self-perceived levels of energy, mood, food cravings and cognitive function', International *Journal of Behavioral Nutrition and Physical Activity*, vol. 13, 2016, p. 113.

Buffey, AJ, Herring, MP, Langley, CK, Donnelly, AE & Carson, BP, 'The acute effects of interrupting prolonged sitting time in adults with standing and light-intensity walking on biomarkers of cardiometabolic health in adults: A systematic review and meta-analysis', *Sports Medicine*, vol. 52, 2022, pp. 1765–1787.

Centers for Disease Control and Prevention, 'Benefits of physical activity', 1 August 2023, cdc.gov/physicalactivity/basics/pa-health/index.htm.

Huang, Y, Chen, Z, Chen, B, Li, Jinze, Yuan, X, Li, Jin, Wang, W, Dai, T, Chen, H, Wang, Y, Wang, R, Wang, P, Guo, J, Dong, Q, Liu, C, Wei, Q, Cao, D & Liu, L, 'Dietary sugar consumption and health: Umbrella review, *BMJ*, vol. 381, 2023, e071609.

Mantantzis, K, Schlaghecken, F, Sünram-Lea, SI & Maylor, EA, 'Sugar rush or sugar crash? A meta-analysis of carbohydrate effects on mood', *Neuroscience & Biobehavioral Reviews*, vol. 101, 2019, pp. 45–67.

O'Callaghan, F, Muurlink, O & Reid, N, 'Effects of caffeine on sleep quality and daytime functioning', *Risk Management and Healthcare Policy*, vol. 11, 2018, pp. 263–271.

Pink, DH, *When: The scientific secrets of perfect timing*, Text, Melbourne, 2018.

Rhee, H & Kim, S, 'Effects of breaks on regaining vitality at work: An empirical comparison of "conventional" and "smart phone" breaks', *Computers in Human Behavior*, vol. 57, 2016, pp. 160–167.

Ricci, JA, Chee, E, Lorandeau, AL & Berger, J, 'Fatigue in the U.S. workforce: Prevalence and implications for lost productive work time' *Journal of Occupational and Environmental Medicine*, vol. 49, no. 1, 2007, pp. 1–10.

Sadeghniiat-Haghighi, K & Yazdi, Z, 'Fatigue management in the workplace', *Industrial Psychiatry Journal*, vol. 24, no. 1, 2015, pp. 12–7.

Sianoja, M, Kinnunen, U, de Bloom, J, Korpela, K & Geurts, S, 'Recovery during lunch breaks: Testing long-term relations with energy levels at work', *Scandinavian Journal of Work and Organizational Psychology*, vol. 1, no. 1, 2016, p. 7.

Chapter 12 | Do your research

Allen, MS, Walter, EE & Swann, C, 'Sedentary behaviour and risk of anxiety: A systematic review and meta-analysis', *Journal of Affective Disorders*, vol. 242, 2018, pp. 5–13.

Australian Bureau of Statistics, *Physical activity*, 21 March 2022, abs.gov.au/statistics/health/health-conditions-and-risks/physical-activity/latest-release.

Bristot, V, Poletto, G, Pereira, DMR, Hauck, M, Schneider, IJC & Aguiar Jr, ASA, 'The effects of exercise on circulating endocannabinoid levels—a protocol for a systematic review and meta-analysis', *Systematic Reviews*, vol. 11, 2022, p. 98.

Brown, HE, Ryde, GC, Gilson, ND, Burton, NW & Brown, WJ, 'Objectively measured sedentary behavior and physical activity in office employees: Relationships with presenteeism', *Journal of Occupational and Environmental Medicine*, vol. 55, no. 8, 2013, pp. 945–953.

Castillo, L, 'Exercise and work productivity statistics [fresh research]', Gitnux, 15 October 2023, blog.gitnux.com/exercise-and-work-productivity-statistics.

Coulson, JC, McKenna, J & Field, M, 'Exercising at work and self-reported work performance', *International Journal of Workplace Health Management*, vol. 1, no. 3, 2008, pp. 176–197.

de Oliveira, C, Saka, M, Bone, L & Jacobs, R, 'The role of mental health on workplace productivity: A critical review of the literature', *Applied Health Economics and Health Policy*, vol. 21, 2023, pp. 167–193.

Guthold, R, Stevens, GA, Riley, LM & Bull, FC, 'Global trends in insufficient physical activity among adolescents: a pooled analysis of 298 population-based surveys with 1·6 million participants', *The Lancet*, vol. 4, no. 1, 2019, pp. 23–35.

Healy, GN & Goode, AD, 'Workplace programmes aimed at limiting occupational sitting', *Sedentary Behaviour Epidemiology*, Springer, Cham, 2018, pp. 445–457.

Koinig, I & Diehl, S, 'Healthy leadership and workplace health promotion as a pre-requisite for organizational health', *International Journal of Environmental Research and Public Health*, vol. 18, no. 17, 2021, p. 9260.

Medibank Private, *Sick at Work: The cost of presenteeism to your business and the Australian economy*, Medibank Research, Brisbane, 2011.

National Heart Foundation of Australia, *Blueprint for an Active Australia* (3rd ed.), 2019, accessed 1 November 2023, heartfoundation.org.au/getmedia/6c33122b-475c-4531-8c26-7e7a7b0eb7c1/Blueprint-For-An-Active-Australia.pdf.

National Preventative Health Taskforce, *Australia: The healthiest country by 2020*, Commonwealth of Australia, Canberra, 30 June 2009.

Oswald, AJ, Proto, E & Sgroi, D, 'Happiness and productivity', *Journal of Labor Economics*, vol. 33, no. 4, 2015, pp. 789–822.

Patterson, R, McNamara, E, Tainio, M, de Sá, TH, Smith, AD, Sharp, SJ, Edwards, P, Woodcock, J, Brage, S & Wijndaele, K, 'Sedentary behaviour and risk of all-cause, cardiovascular and cancer mortality, and incident type 2 diabetes: A systematic review and dose response meta-analysis', *European Journal of Epidemiology*, vol. 33, no. 9, 2018, pp. 811–829.

PricewaterhouseCoopers, 'Creating a mentally healthy workplace: a return on investment analysis', 2014, headsup.org.au/docs/default-source/resources/beyondblue_workplaceroi_finalreport_may-2014.pdf.

Robison, J, 'What leaders must do next', *Gallup*, 11 June 2009, news.gallup.com/businessjournal/120791/leaders-next.aspx.

Standards Council of Canada, *Psychological health and safety in the workplace: Prevention, promotion, and guidance to staged implementation*, CSA Group, Toronto, 2013.

University of Warwick, 'New study shows we work harder when we are happy', accessed 27 October 2023, warwick.ac.uk/newsandevents/pressreleases/new_study_shows.

World Health Organization, 'Workers' health: Global plan of action', World Health Organization, Geneva, 23 May 2007, who.int/gb/ebwha/pdf_files/WHA60/A60_R26-en.pdf.

World Health Organization, *WHO Guidelines on Physical Activity and Sedentary Behaviour*, World Health Organization, Geneva, 2020, iris.who.int/bitstream/handle/10665/336656/9789240015128-eng.pdf.

Chapter 13 | Be a role model

The Daily Mile UK, 'What is the Daily Mile', accessed 27 October 2023, thedailymile.co.uk/what-is-the-daily-mile.

Sinek, S, 'Leadership is not about being in charge. Leadership is about taking care of those in your charge.', LinkedIn, 2021, linkedin.com/posts/simonsinek_leadership-is-not-about-being-in-charge-activity-6795194053433540608-CiRs.

Chapter 15 | Design your roadmap

Bellew, B, *Primary prevention of chronic disease in Australia through interventions in the workplace setting: A rapid review*, The Sax Institute, August 2008, saxinstitute.org.au/wp-content/uploads/29_Primary-prevention-chronic-disease....workplace-setting.pdf.